**TEACHER'S PET PUBLICATIONS**

LITPLAN TEACHER PACK
for
The Picture of Dorian Gray
based on the book by
Oscar Wilde

Written by
Susan R. Woodward

© 2008 Teacher's Pet Publications
All Rights Reserved

Copyright Teacher's Pet Publications 2008

Only the student materials in this unit plan (such as worksheets, study questions, and tests) may be reproduced multiple times for use in the purchaser's classroom.

For any additional copyright questions, contact Teacher's Pet Publications.

www.tpet.com

TABLE OF CONTENTS - *The Picture of Dorian Gray*

About The Author	4
Introduction	5
Unit Objectives	7
Reading Assignment Sheet	8
Unit Outline	9
Study Questions (Short Answer)	13
Quiz/Study Questions (Multiple Choice)	24
Pre-reading Vocabulary Worksheets	49
Lesson One (Introductory Lesson)	77
Non-fiction Assignment Sheet	92
Oral Reading Evaluation Form	105
Writing Assignment #1	112
Writing Evaluation Form	113
Group Project	123
Writing Assignment #2	124
Extra Writing Assignments/Discussion ?s	134
Vocabulary Review Activities	136
Writing Assignment #3	140
Unit Review Activities	147
Unit Tests	153
Unit Resource Materials	211
Vocabulary Resource Materials	229

ABOUT THE AUTHOR

Oscar Wilde

Oscar Fingal O'Flahertie Wills Wilde was born October 16, 1854 in Dublin, Ireland to Sir William Wilde, a renowned ear and eye surgeon, and Jane Francesca Elgee, a writer and Irish nationalist. Wilde was primarily a playwright, poet, and short story writer; however, his only novel, *The Picture of Dorian Gray,* is probably one of his most memorable works. Oscar Wilde's father, best remembered for his dedicated medical care in Dublin's poorest neighborhoods, also published books on archeology and folklore.

After being home schooled by his mother until the age of nine, Oscar Wilde entered Portora Royal School in 1864. In 1871, Wilde entered Trinity College, Dublin and proved himself to be an outstanding student. He won the Berkely Gold Medal, which is the highest award available for students of classical studies, particularly languages, history, literature, and art. As a result, Oscar Wilde was awarded a scholarship to Magdalen College in Oxford, England where he continued his study of the classics and became part of the Aesthetic movement. This movement was characterized by an excessive appreciation of the arts and the idea that life had to be lived intensely, following an ideal of beauty. The characteristics of Lord Henry Wotton and Dorian Gray in Wilde's only novel are prime examples of those who live life according to the standards of the Aesthetic movement. While at Magdalen College, Wilde won the 1878 Newdigate Prize for his poem "Ravenna." He graduated in November 1878 with a double first (highest honors in two areas of study) in classical moderations and Literae Humaniores, or "greats" in classical literature.

Wilde returned to Ireland after graduating from Magdalen. It was in his hometown of Dublin where he met and fell in love with Florence Balcombe. When she did not return his love and, instead, became engaged to Bram Stoker (author of *Dracula*), Wilde vowed to leave Ireland forever. He spent the next six years on a lecture tour that took him to London, Paris, and parts of the United States. It was while he was in London that Wilde met Constance Lloyd, the daughter of Queen's Counsel Horace Lloyd, and they married May 29, 1884. As the daughter of the Queen's Counsel (the Queen's personal lawyer), Constance was given a generous allowance by her father, allowing her and her new husband Oscar Wilde a comfortably luxurious lifestyle. The couple had two sons, Cyril (1885) and Vyvyan (1886).

It was this comfortable lifestyle that allowed Wilde the leisure time to engage in activities that led to a terrible scandal surrounding Wilde's alleged homosexuality. In May 1895, this scandal culminated in Wilde being sentenced to two years of hard labor for "gross indecency." The shame of this public humiliation led Wilde's wife Constance to change her name and Wilde's sons' names to "Holland." She died in Italy in 1989 following spinal surgery. Wilde's son, Cyril was killed in France during World War I. Vyvyan also served in the war and went on to become an author and translator. Merlin Holland, Vyvyan's son, edited and published several works about his grandfather, Oscar Wilde.

INTRODUCTION - *The Picture of Dorian Gray*

This LitPlan has been designed to develop students' reading, writing, thinking, and language skills through exercises and activities related to *The Picture of Dorian Gray*. It includes 21 lessons supported by extra resource materials.

The **introductory lesson** introduces students to the nineteenth century gothic novel and the concept of the "doppelganger" or "evil twin." Following the introductory activity, students are given a transition to explain how the activity relates to the novel they are about to read. Following the transition, students are given the materials they will be using during the unit. At the end of the lesson, students begin the pre-reading work for the first reading assignment.

The **reading assignments** are approximately thirty pages each; some are a little shorter while others are a little longer. Students have approximately 15 minutes of pre-reading work to do prior to each reading assignment. This pre-reading work involves reviewing the study questions for the assignment and doing some vocabulary work for selected words they will encounter in their reading.

The **study guide questions** are fact-based questions; students can find the answers to these questions right in the text. These questions come in two formats: short answer or multiple choice. The best use of these materials is probably to use the short answer version of the questions as study guides for students (since answers will be more complete) and to use the multiple choice version for occasional quizzes.

The **vocabulary work** is intended to enrich students' vocabularies as well as to aid in the students' understanding of the book. Prior to each reading assignment, students will complete a two-part worksheet for selected vocabulary words in the upcoming reading assignment. Part I focuses on students' use of general knowledge and contextual clues. The sentence in which the word appears in the text is given, and students are asked to write down what they think the words mean. Part II nails down the definitions of the words by giving students dictionary definitions of the words and having students match the words to the correct definitions based on the words' contextual usage. Students should then have an understanding of the words when they meet them in the text.

After each reading assignment, students formulate answers for the study guide questions. Discussion of these questions serves as a **review** of the most important events and ideas presented in the reading assignments.

After students complete reading the work, there is a **vocabulary review** lesson which pulls together all of the fragmented vocabulary lists for the reading assignments and gives students a review of all of the words they have studied.

Following the vocabulary review, a lesson is devoted to the **extra discussion questions/writing assignments**. These questions focus on interpretation, critical analysis and personal response, employing a variety of thinking skills and adding to the students' understanding of the novel.

There is a **group theme project** in this unit. Student groups will create scandal sheets (a la *The National Enquirer*) referencing characters from Wilde's *The Picture of Dorian Gray*.

There are three **writing assignments** in this unit, each with the purpose of informing, persuading, or expressing personal opinions. In Writing Assignment #1, students will research topics that had captivated Dorian Gray's attention in his exploration of the senses. In Writing Assignment #2, as a part of the group project, students will write two newspaper articles about a character in the novel. Finally, in Writing Assignment #3, students select one of three quotations and determine whether or not they agree with the main idea of the quotation with relation to *The Picture of Dorian Gray*.

There is a **non-fiction reading assignment**. Students must read non-fiction materials to gather information about lives of the rich and famous. In particular, students will research those who have so much money that they do not know what to do with it or with themselves, and whose names and faces are continuously linked to scandal. This research will then be tied in with the nineteenth century concept of "dandyism" explored in Wilde's novel.

The **review lesson** pulls together all of the aspects of the unit. The teacher is given choices of activities or games to use which all serve the same basic function of reviewing all of the information presented in the unit.

The **unit test** comes in two formats: multiple choice or short answer. As a convenience, two different tests for each format have been included. There is also an advanced short answer unit test for advanced students.

There are additional **support materials** included with this unit. The **Unit Resource Materials** section includes suggestions for an in-class library, crossword and word search puzzles related to the novel, and extra worksheets. There is a list of **bulletin board ideas** which gives the teacher suggestions for bulletin boards to go along with this unit. In addition, there is a list of **extra class activities** the teacher could choose from to enhance the unit or as a substitution for an exercise the teacher might feel is inappropriate for his/her class. **Answer keys** are located directly after the **reproducible student materials** throughout the unit. The **Vocabulary Resource Materials** section includes similar worksheets and games to reinforce the vocabulary words.

The **level** of this unit can be varied depending upon the criteria on which the individual assignments are graded, the teacher's expectations of his/her students in class discussions, and the formats chosen for the study guides, quizzes and test. If teachers have other ideas/activities they wish to use, they can usually easily be inserted prior to the review lesson.

The student materials may be reproduced for use in the teacher's classroom without infringement of copyrights. No other portion of this unit may be reproduced without the written consent of Teacher's Pet Publications, Inc.

UNIT OBJECTIVES *The Picture of Dorian Gray*

1. Through reading Oscar Wilde's *The Picture of Dorian Gray*, students will gain a better understanding of the Gothic tradition in literature, particularly the idea of "the doppelganger" or "evil twin."

2. Students will demonstrate their understanding of the text on four levels: factual, interpretive, critical and personal.

3. Students will become familiar with Carl Jung's concept of the "shadow" through some of his writings on the collective unconscious.

4. Students will be given the opportunity to practice reading aloud and silently to improve their skills in each area.

5. Students will answer questions to demonstrate their knowledge and understanding of the main events and characters in *The Picture of Dorian Gray* as they relate to the author's theme development.

6. Students will enrich their vocabularies and improve their understanding of the novel through the vocabulary lessons prepared for use in conjunction with the novel.

7. The writing assignments in this unit are geared to several purposes:

    a. To have students demonstrate their abilities to inform, to persuade, or to express their own personal ideas

    Note: Students will demonstrate the ability to write effectively to inform by developing and organizing facts to convey information. Students will demonstrate the ability to write effectively to persuade by selecting and organizing relevant information, establishing an argumentative purpose, and by designing an appropriate strategy for an identified audience. Students will demonstrate the ability to write effectively to express personal ideas by selecting a form and its appropriate elements.

    b. To check the students' reading comprehension

    c. To make students think about the ideas presented by the novel

    d. To encourage logical thinking

    e. To provide an opportunity to practice good grammar and improve students' use of the English language.

8. Students will read aloud, report, and participate in large and small group discussions to improve their public speaking and personal interaction skills.

READING ASSIGNMENTS *The Picture of Dorian Gray*

Date Assigned	Assignment	Completion Date
	Assignment 1 Chapters 1-2	
	Assignment 2 Chapters 3-4	
	Assignment 3 Chapters 5-6	
	Assignment 4 Chapters 7-8	
	Assignment 5 Chapters 9-10	
	Assignment 6 Chapters 11-12	
	Assignment 7 Chapters 13-14	
	Assignment 8 Chapters 15-16	
	Assignment 9 Chapters 17-18	
	Assignment 10 Chapters 19-20	

UNIT OUTLINE *The Picture of Dorian Gray*

1 Introduction Gothic Literature PVR 1-2	2 Study ? 1-2 Non-fiction Assignment PVR 3-4	3 Study ? 3-4 Critical Thinking Skills Quiz PVR 5-6	4 Study ? 5-6 Characterization PVR 7-8	5 Study ? 7-8 Quiz Oral Reading PVR 9-10
6 Study ? 9-10 Non-fiction Presentations PVR 11-12	7 Study ? 11-12 Quiz Writting Assignment #1 PVR 13-14	8 Study ? 13-14 Collective Unconscious PVR 15-16	9 Study ? 15-16 Quiz Oral Reading PVR 17-18	10 Study ? 17-18 Introdcution to Writing Assignment #2 PVR 19-20
11 Study ? 19-20 Quiz False Friend	12 Writing Assignment #2 Work	13 Vocabulary Review	14 Extra Discussion Questions	15 Writing Assignment #3
16 Peer Editing	17 Group Project Work	18 Group Presentations	19 Group Presentations	20 Unit Review
21 Unit Test				

Key: P = Preview Study Questions   V = Vocabulary Work   R = Read

STUDY GUIDE QUESTIONS

STUDY GUIDE QUESTIONS *The Picture of Dorian Gray*

Assignment 1
Chapters 1-2
1. Who is Basil Hallward?
2. What completely captures Lord Henry Wotton's attention when he visits Hallward's studio?
3. What reason does Basil give for not wanting to exhibit his painting of Dorian Gray?
4. What does Basil believe are the only two eras of importance in the world's history?
5. Basil believes that his landscape painting is the finest work he's ever done. To what does he attribute this success?
6. Why doesn't Basil want to introduce Lord Henry to Dorian Gray?
7. What does Lord Henry claim is "the aim of life"?
8. According to Lord Henry, what is "the only way to get rid of a temptation"?
9. What does Dorian Gray so desperately wish for that he "would give [his] soul" to have it come true?
10. To what does Basil attribute Dorian's negative reaction to his painting?

Assignment 2
Chapters 3-4
1. What happened to Dorian Gray's father?
2. What exercise does Lord Henry find "terribly enthralling"?
3. What advice does Lord Henry give the Duchess when she asks how she can become young again?
4. Who claims that Lord Henry is "extremely dangerous" yet still wishes to hear more of Henry's "philosophy of pleasure"?
5. When Dorian Gray is reminded that he promised to visit Basil Hallward, where does Dorian go instead?
6. Who is Victoria?
7. With whom does Dorian Gray fall in love?
8. What does Lord Henry tell Dorian Gray is "the real secret of life"?
9. To where does Dorian want Henry and Basil to accompany him?
10. What news is in the telegram that Lord Henry receives from Dorian?

Assignment 3
Chapters 5-6
1. What does Mr. Isaacs do to help Sibyl and her family?
2. By what name does Sibyl Vane know Dorian Gray?
3. What does Jim demand to know from his mother before he leaves for Australia?
4. What threat does Jim make regarding "Prince Charming"?
5. What does Lord Henry say is the "real drawback to marriage"?
6. How does Dorian describe the details of his engagement to Sibyl Vane?

7. What does it mean to be "good," according to Lord Henry?
8. What does Lord Henry tell Dorian Gray that he represents to the young man?

Assignment 4
Chapters 7-8
1. When Lord Henry and Basil accompany Dorian to the theatre, what happens to make Dorian angry?
2. What explanation does Sibyl Vane offer Dorian regarding her performance?
3. What is Dorian's reaction to Sibyl's explanation for her poor performance?
4. After he breaks off his relationship with Sibyl, what does Dorian notice about the painting Basil had done of him?
5. What does Dorian Gray realize when he sees the changes in the painting?
6. What news is in Lord Henry's letter that Dorian does not open?
7. What choice does Dorian Gray make after Lord Henry points out how fortunate Dorian is that someone loved him so much as to kill herself for him?
8. What does Dorian believe would be a real pleasure to watch?

Assignment 5
Chapters 9-10
1. Where does Basil believe Dorian had gone after learning the news about Sibyl?
2. Where does Dorian go the evening he learns of Sibyl's fate?
3. Who does Basil blame for the changes in Dorian?
4. Dorian threatens never to speak to Basil again. Why?
5. What does Basil want to do with the portrait of Dorian he painted?
6. Who is Mrs. Leaf?
7. Where does Dorian Gray decide to hide the painting?
8. What does the coroner give as the official cause of Sibyl Vane's death?
9. What does Lord Henry send to Dorian that completely fascinates him?
10. Why is Dorian late meeting Lord Henry for dinner?

Assignment 6
Chapters 11-12
1. What becomes a huge influence over Dorian Gray's life?
2. Why do people tend to disbelieve the rumors about Dorian Gray?
3. What does Dorian Gray do once or twice every month during the winter, and each Wednesday evening while the season lasts?
4. What are some of the activities or interests that capture Dorian Gray's attention in his study of the senses?
5. What is the Duke of Berwick's reaction when Dorian Gray is "brought by a friend into the smoking room of the Churchill"?
6. To what city does Basil tell Dorian he plans to travel?
7. What is it that Basil wishes to speak to Dorian about before leaving?

8. What sort of fate have many of Dorian's acquaintances met?
9. What does Basil claim that he would have to see before he could believe anything he's heard about Dorian's activities?
10. Where does Dorian take Basil so that the artist may see the "diary of [his] life"?

Assignment 7
Chapters 13-14
1. What does Basil see when he looks at the portrait he painted of Dorian Gray?
2. What does Basil implore Dorian to do after seeing the condition of the painting?
3. What does Dorian Gray do to Basil?
4. Where does Dorian hide Basil's belongings?
5. What does Dorian do to provide himself with an alibi regarding Basil's death?
6. As Dorian sketched, what seems to appear in all of his drawings?
7. Who does Dorian send his servant to fetch on the morning after Basil's death?
8. In what particular field of study does Alan Campbell specialize?
9. What request does Dorian Gray make of Alan Campbell?
10. Why does Alan Campbell agree to do as Dorian asks?

Assignment 8
Chapters 15-16
1. What is Dorian's mood when he attends Lady Narborough's party?
2. Why does Lady Narborough seem to hate visiting her daughter and son-in-law?
3. Whom does Lady Narbourough accuse of being "extremely wicked"?
4. What does Lord Henry ask Dorian at Lady Narbourough's party that makes Dorian nervous?
5. What "things that were dangerous" does Dorian believe had to be dealt with immediately upon arriving home from Lady Narborough's dinner party?
6. What words did Lord Henry say the first day he met Dorian that now repeatedly play through Dorian's mind?
7. Though Dorian believes that forgiveness for his sins is impossible, what is "possible still"?
8. What former friend does Dorian Gray see at the opium house?
9. Who is the drunken sailor who accuses Dorian Gray in the street?
10. Why doesn't the drunken sailor shoot Dorian Gray?

Assignment 9
Chapters 17-18
1. With what does Lord Henry have "one quarrel"?
2. When Gladys tells Lord Henry he values beauty far too much, what is his response?
3. According to Lord Henry what three things, "have made . . . England what she is?
4. What is Lord Henry's answer when the Duchess asks him to describe women?
5. What does Dorian believe he had seen through the window of the conservatory?

6. What does Dorian Gray blame for raising "such fearful phantoms" that keep him in his house for three days?
7. What does Dorian beg Sir Geoffrey Clouston not to do?
8. What happens that Dorian Gray proclaims to be a "bad omen"?
9. Who is the man in the thicket?

Assignment 10
Chapters 19-20
1. What does Dorian promise that he will do in the future?
2. Who is Hetty?
3. Although Dorian believes he has done right by Hetty, what does Lord Henry say will be the result of Dorian's great renunciation?
4. What becomes of Alan Campbell?
5. What does Dorian tell Lord Henry that Henry immediately dismisses as impossible to believe?
6. What does Dorian claim is "a terrible reality . . . [that] . . . can be bought, and sold, and bartered away"?
7. What is Dorian "tired of hearing . . . now"?
8. What does Dorian believe should be the prayer of a man to a most just God instead of "Forgive us our sins"?
9. Why does Dorian go to look at his portrait while thinking of Hetty Merton?
10. What happens to Dorian Gray?

STUDY GUIDE QUESTIONS ANSWER KEY *The Picture of Dorian Gray*

Assignment 1
Chapters 1-2

1. Who is Basil Hallward?
   He is a London artist who paints the portrait of young Dorian Gray.

2. What completely captures Lord Henry Wotton's attention when he visits Hallward's studio?
   Lord Wotton is fascinated by Basil's subject for the painting, a beautiful young man named Dorian Gray.

3. What reason does Basil give for not wanting to exhibit his painting of Dorian Gray?
   Basil feels that he has put too much of his own self into the painting, and it reveals the secrets of his soul.

4. What does Basil believe are the only two eras of importance in the world's history?
   He believes that the appearance of a new medium for art and the appearance of a new personality for art are the only two eras of importance in the world's history.

5. Basil believes that his landscape painting is the finest work he's ever done. To what does he attribute this success?
   Dorian Gray was sitting beside Basil when he painted the landscape. Basil credits "some subtle influence" from Dorian's presence to the success of the work.

6. Why doesn't Basil want to introduce Lord Henry to Dorian Gray?
   Basil is afraid that Lord Henry will be a negative influence on the young Dorian.

7. What does Lord Henry claim is "the aim of life"?
   Lord Henry claims that self-development is the "aim of life."

8. According to Lord Henry, what is "the only way to get rid of a temptation"?
   Lord Henry believes that "the only way to get rid of a temptation is to yield to it."

9. What does Dorian Gray so desperately wish for that he "would give [his] soul" to have it come true?
   Dorian wishes that his portrait would age and that he would remain young and untouched by the ugliness of life.

10. To what does Basil attribute Dorian's negative reaction to his painting?
    Basil attributes Dorian's reaction to Lord Henry's negative influence.

Assignment 2
Chapters 3-4

1. What happened to Dorian Gray's father?
   Dorian's father was killed in a duel. It was rumored, but never proved, that this duel was set up by Dorian's grandfather because he despised the young man who had married his daughter.

2. What exercise does Lord Henry find "terribly enthralling"?
   Lord Henry is enthralled with the exercise of influence.

3. What advice does Lord Henry give the Duchess when she asks how she can become young again?
   He tells her that the secret of being young is to repeat the follies of her youth.

4. Who claims that Lord Henry is "extremely dangerous" yet still wishes to hear more of Henry's "philosophy of pleasure"?
   Mr. Erskine feels this way about Lord Henry.

5. When Dorian Gray is reminded that he promised to visit Basil Hallward, where does Dorian go instead?
   Dorian chooses to go to the park with Lord Henry instead of keeping his promise to visit Basil.
6. Who is Victoria?
   Victoria is Lord Henry Wotton's wife.
7. With whom does Dorian Gray fall in love?
   Dorian falls in love with an actress, Sibyl Vane.
8. What does Lord Henry tell Dorian Gray is "the real secret of life"?
   Lord Henry tells Dorian that "the real secret of life" is the search for beauty.
9. To where does Dorian want Henry and Basil to accompany him?
   Dorian wants Henry and Basil to come to the theatre to see Sibyl Vane, Dorian's love-interest, play Juliet.
10. What news is in the telegram that Lord Henry receives from Dorian?
    Dorian sends a telegram to Lord Henry announcing his engagement to Sibyl Vane.

Assignment 3
Chapters 5-6
1. What does Mr. Isaacs do to help Sibyl and her family?
   Mr. Isaacs advanced them 50 pounds to pay off their debts and to buy James a proper outfit.
2. By what name does Sibyl Vane know Dorian Gray?
   Sibyl only knows Dorian as "Prince Charming."
3. What does Jim demand to know from his mother before he leaves for Australia?
   Jim demands to know whether or not his mother was ever married to his father. (He learns that she wasn't.)
4. What threat does Jim make regarding "Prince Charming"?
   Jim swears that if "Prince Charming" ever hurts Sibyl, he will kill him.
5. What does Lord Henry say is the "real drawback to marriage"?
   Lord Henry claims that marriage makes people unselfish and that unselfish people are colorless and lack individuality.
6. How does Dorian describe the details of his engagement to Sibyl Vane?
   They'd kissed backstage after one of her performances. Dorian told Sibyl that he loved her, and she said that she was unworthy to be his wife. He'd not actually proposed, but he considered himself engaged to her.
7. What does it mean to be "good," according to Lord Henry?
   To be good is to be in harmony with oneself.
8. What does Lord Henry tell Dorian Gray that he represents to the young man?
   Lord Henry says that he represents all the sins that Dorian has not had the courage to commit.

Assignment 4
Chapters 7-8
1. When Lord Henry and Basil accompany Dorian to the theatre, what happens to make Dorian angry?
   Sibyl's performance is terrible. Lord Henry and Basil leave during the show.
2. What explanation does Sibyl Vane offer Dorian regarding her performance?
   She no longer desires to live the lives of her characters, and she wishes to live in the real world with Dorian. She now sees the actors on the stage and not the characters she used to see. This reality has spoiled her acting.
3. What is Dorian's reaction to Sibyl's explanation for her poor performance?
   Dorian says that he is no longer in love with her, and he will never see her again.
4. After he breaks off his relationship with Sibyl, what does Dorian notice about the painting Basil had done of him?
   The painting has changed, and on the face of the painting "there was a touch of cruelty in the mouth."
5. What does Dorian Gray realize when he sees the changes in the painting?
   Dorian realizes how cruel he has been to Sibyl Vane, and he vows that he will make it up to her.
6. What news is in Lord Henry's letter that Dorian does not open?
   Lord Henry's note says he has learned that Sibyl Vane died in an incident at the theater.
7. What choice does Dorian Gray make after Lord Henry points out how fortunate Dorian is that someone loved him so much as to kill herself for him?
   Dorian chooses to follow his passions and to allow the painting "to bear the burden of his shame."
8. What does Dorian believe would be a real pleasure to watch?
   Dorian believes that it would be a real pleasure to watch the painting change while he physically remains the same.

Assignment 5
Chapters 9-10
1. Where does Basil believe Dorian had gone after learning the news about Sibyl?
   Basil believes that Dorian went to comfort Sibyl's mother after the tragedy of Sibyl's death.
2. Where does Dorian go the evening he learns of Sibyl's fate?
   He goes to the opera with Lord Henry.
3. Who does Basil blame for the changes in Dorian?
   Basil blames Lord Henry for the negative changes in Dorian.
4. Dorian threatens never to speak to Basil again. Why?
   Dorian doesn't want Basil to see the painting, so he threatens never to speak to Basil again if Basil looks at it.
5. What does Basil want to do with the portrait of Dorian he painted?
   Basil wants to exhibit the portrait in Paris.
6. Who is Mrs. Leaf?
   Mrs. Leaf is Dorian Gray's housekeeper.
7. Where does Dorian Gray decide to hide the painting?
   Dorian decides to move the painting into an old schoolroom at the top of his house and keep the painting under lock and key.

8. What does the coroner give as the official cause of Sibyl Vane's death?
   The coroner's official report is that Sibyl Vane met her "death by misadventure." It was officially proclaimed an accidental death.
9. What does Lord Henry send to Dorian that completely fascinates him?
   Lord Henry sends Dorian a book about a man who lived his life completely by fulfilling his senses.
10. Why is Dorian late meeting Lord Henry for dinner?
    Dorian gets so caught up in the book, he is late for dinner.

Assignment 6
Chapters 11-12
1. What becomes a huge influence over Dorian Gray's life?
   The book that Lord Henry gave Dorian has a huge influence over Dorian's behavior. He is so caught up in it, he purchases nine copies of it and has them bound in various colors to match his changing moods.
2. Why do people tend to disbelieve the rumors about Dorian Gray?
   Because the portrait in his upstairs room absorbed all the aging and marks of sin, Dorian's youthful beauty keeps people from believing the worst about him.
3. What does Dorian Gray do once or twice every month during the winter, and each Wednesday evening while the season lasts?
   Dorian hosts lavish parties complete with extravagant food and music. It is at these parties that he exerts his influence over impressionable young people.
4. What are some of the activities or interests that capture Dorian Gray's attention in his study of the senses?
   Dorian, over a period of several years, delves into many areas of interest. Dorian studies embroidered clothing, tapestries, jewels, perfumes, the ritual of Roman Catholicism, mysticism, and music. When he gets bored with one topic, he moves on to the next.
5. What is the Duke of Berwick's reaction when Dorian Gray is "brought by a friend into the smoking room of the Churchill"?
   When Dorian comes into the room, the Duke of Berwick walks out.
6. To what city does Basil tell Dorian he plans to travel?
   Basil tells Dorian that he is leaving for Paris for a six months' stay.
7. What is it that Basil wishes to speak to Dorian about before leaving?
   Basil wants to know the truth about the terrible rumors that are going around town surrounding Dorian's moral character.
8. What sort of fate have many of Dorian's acquaintances met?
   Those who were closest to Dorian have lost their respectable reputations in society.
9. What does Basil claim that he would have to see before he could believe anything he's heard about Dorian's activities?
   Basil claims that he would have to see Dorian's soul before he could believe any of the rumors he's heard about Dorian.
10. Where does Dorian take Basil so that the artist may see the "diary of [his] life"?
    Dorian takes Basil upstairs to the locked schoolroom where the painting is kept. He intends to show it to the artist.

Assignment 7
Chapters 13-14

1. What does Basil see when he looks at the portrait he painted of Dorian Gray?
   Basil sees an aging man who had the look of a satyr. The cruelty of the mouth and the evil in it's eyes horrifies him.

2. What does Basil implore Dorian to do after seeing the condition of the painting?
   Basil begs Dorian to get on his knees and pray to God for forgiveness of his sins.

3. What does Dorian Gray do to Basil?
   Dorian viciously stabs Basil in the neck with an artist's knife.

4. Where does Dorian hide Basil's belongings?
   He hides them in a secret compartment behind the wainscoting.

5. What does Dorian do to provide himself with an alibi regarding Basil's death?
   Dorian goes outside and bangs on his door to awaken his servants. In doing so his servants will provide him with an alibi that he returned home after Basil had gone.

6. As Dorian sketches, what seems to appear in all of his drawings?
   Basil Hallward's face begins to appear in all of his sketches.

7. Who does Dorian send his servant to fetch on the morning after Basil's death?
   Dorian sends his servant to fetch Alan Campbell, a former friend of Dorian.

8. In what particular field of study does Alan Campbell specialize?
   Alan Campbell specializes in the field of science, particularly chemistry.

9. What request does Dorian Gray make of Alan Campbell?
   Dorian asks Alan Campbell to dispose of Basil's body through the use of chemicals and fire.

10. Why does Alan Campbell agree to do as Dorian asks?
    Dorian Gray blackmails Alan Campbell with some deed from his past when he and Dorian had been friends. Dorian threatens to ruin Alan's reputation if he doesn't do it.

Assignment 8
Chapters 15-16

1. What is Dorian's mood when he attends Lady Narborough's party?
   He is surprisingly calm despite what had happened with Basil.

2. Why does Lady Narborough seem to hate visiting her daughter and son-in-law?
   She thinks that living in the country is too boring.

3. Whom does Lady Narbourough accuse of being "extremely wicked"?
   Lady Narborough accuses Lord Henry of being extremely wicked.

4. What does Lord Henry ask Dorian at Lady Narbourough's party that makes Dorian nervous?
   Lord Henry asks Dorian where he went after leaving early the night before.

5. What "things that were dangerous" does Dorian believe had to be dealt with immediately upon arriving home from Lady Narborough's dinner party?
   Dorian feels that he needs to immediately destroy all evidence that Basil had returned to the house, so he buries Basil's ulster and bag.

6. What words did Lord Henry say the first day he met Dorian that now repeatedly play through Dorian's mind?
   On the day they had met, Lord Henry told Dorian that one could "cure the soul by means of the senses and the senses by means of the soul."

7. Though Dorian believes that forgiveness for his sins is impossible, what is "possible still"?
   Although Dorian feels he cannot be forgiven for his sins, he could still obtain forgetfulness through drugs.
8. What former friend does Dorian Gray see at the opium house?
   Dorian meets Adrian Singleton, a man who had once been a close friend, but whose life was ruined through his association with Dorian.
9. Who is the drunken sailor who accuses Dorian Gray in the street?
   The drunken sailor is James Vane, Sibyl Vane's older brother, who had vowed to kill "Prince Charming" if he ever hurt his sister.
10. Why doesn't the drunken sailor shoot Dorian Gray?
    Dorian tells James to look at him closely under a street lamp and see that, with his youthful looks, he could not have possibly been the man who caused Sibyl Vane to commit suicide eighteen years earlier.

Assignment 9
Chapters 17-18
1. With what does Lord Henry have "one quarrel"?
   Lord Henry's one quarrel is with words. He believes that society has "lost the faculty of giving lovely names to things."
2. When Gladys tells Lord Henry he values beauty far too much, what is his response?
   Lord Henry admits he thinks it is better to be beautiful than to be good--but acknowledges it is better to be good than ugly.
3. According to Lord Henry what three things, "have made . . . England what she is?
   Lord Henry says, "Beer, the Bible, and the seven deadly virtues have made our England what she is."
4. What is Lord Henry's answer when the Duchess asks him to describe women?
   Lord Henry says, "Sphinxes without secrets."
5. What does Dorian believe he had seen through the window of the conservatory?
   Dorian believes he saw the face of James Vane watching him.
6. What does Dorian Gray blame for raising "such fearful phantoms" that keep him in his house for three days?
   He blames his conscience.
7. What does Dorian beg Sir Geoffrey Clouston not to do?
   Dorian begs Sir Geoffrey not to shoot a hare that was jumping into a thicket.
8. What happens that Dorian Gray proclaims to be a "bad omen"?
   Sir Geoffrey ignores Dorian's request not to shoot at the hare. He shoots into the thicket, but there is a man hiding there. Dorian believes that the shooting of this man is a bad omen of things to come.
9. Who is the man in the thicket?
   The man is James Vane, Sibyl Vane's brother. He had been hiding in the thicket intending to kill Dorian.

Assignment 10
<u>Chapters 19-20</u>

1. What does Dorian promise that he will do in the future?
   Dorian promises that he will be good in the future.

2. Who is Hetty?
   Hetty is a young peasant girl with whom Dorian had planned to run away. Once he decides to be "good," Dorian believes that leaving her while she is still pure would be the best thing for her.

3. Although Dorian believes he has done right by Hetty, what does Lord Henry say will be the result of Dorian's great renunciation?
   Lord Henry says that Dorian's jilting of Hetty has probably ruined any chance of Hetty's happiness with any other man.

4. What becomes of Alan Campbell?
   Alan Campbell commits suicide.

5. What does Dorian tell Lord Henry that Henry immediately dismisses as impossible to believe?
   Dorian tells Lord Henry that he killed Basil. Lord Henry thinks this is impossible since a man's sins would show in his face, and Dorian's face is still as beautiful and youthful as the day they met.

6. What does Dorian claim is "a terrible reality . . . [that] . . . can be bought, and sold, and bartered away"?
   Dorian says this about the soul.

7. What is Dorian "tired of hearing . . . now"?
   Dorian is tired of hearing the sound of his own name coming from others.

8. What does Dorian believe should be the prayer of a man to a most just God instead of "Forgive us our sins"?
   He believes that man's prayer to a most just God should be "smite us for our iniquities."

9. Why does Dorian go to look at his portrait while thinking of Hetty Merton?
   Dorian believes that the picture must now be shedding its ugliness since he has decided to become good, and he had committed a "good deed" by leaving Hetty.

10. What happens to Dorian Gray?
    Dorian attempts to destroy the painting by stabbing it. However, when the servants break into the room (after hearing a loud cry of anguish), they find an old decrepit man with a knife in his heart next to a beautiful painting of Dorian Gray. They only recognize the dead man as their master when they see his rings."

MULTIPLE CHOICE STUDY/QUIZ QUESTIONS
The Picture of Dorian Gray

Assignment 1
Chapters 1-2

1. Who is Basil Hallward?
    A. He is the chief constable in London.
    B. He is a young man of great beauty.
    C. He is a London artist who paints the portrait of young Dorian Gray.
    D. He is a wealthy landlord.

2. What completely captures Lord Henry Wotton's attention when he visits Hallward's studio?
    A. He is fascinated with the Duchess who is visiting Basil.
    B. He is fascinated by Basil's subject for a painting, a beautiful young man named Dorian Gray.
    C. He is enamored by a beautiful sunset that he wishes to paint.
    D. He cannot take his eyes off the landscape painting Basil has just completed.

3. What reason does Basil give for not wanting to exhibit his painting of Dorian Gray?
    A. He feels that he has put too much of his own self into the painting, and it reveals the secrets of his soul.
    B. He is afraid others will laugh at the painting's quality.
    C. He painted it for Dorian, and it is not his to exhibit.
    D. He hates the painting and does not want anyone to see it.

4. What does Basil believe are the only two eras of importance in the world's history?
    A. He believes that the appearance of a new medium for art and the appearance of a new personality for art are the most important.
    B. He believes Social Darwinism and the Industrial Revolution of the Nineteenth Century are the most important.
    C. He believes the Ancient Greek civilization and the spread of the Roman Empire are the most important.
    D. He believes the artistic rebirth of the Renaissance and the Transcendental Movement are the most important.

5. Basil believes that his landscape painting is the finest work he's ever done. To what does he attribute this success?
    A. He was blessed by the muses when he painted it.
    B. His love for a beautiful woman inspired him to see the glorious beauty of nature.
    C. Basil had a generous financial benefactor to fund the project.
    D. Dorian Gray was sitting beside Basil when he painted the landscape. Basil credits "some subtle influence" from Dorian's presence to the success of the work.

6. Why doesn't Basil want to introduce Lord Henry to Dorian Gray?
    A. Basil is afraid for Dorian's safety.
    B. Lord Henry is a known thief, and Basil wants to protect Dorian from involvement.
    C. Basil is afraid that Lord Henry will be a negative influence on the young Dorian.
    D. Lord Henry is an evil old man who would ruin Dorian's reputation.

7. What does Lord Henry claim is "the aim of life"?
    A. Lord Henry claims that truth is the "aim of life."
    B. Lord Henry claims that good deeds are the "aim of life."
    C. Lord Henry claims that self-development is the "aim of life."
    D. Lord Henry claims the pursuit of happiness is the "aim of life."

8. According to Lord Henry, what is "the only way to get rid of a temptation"?
    A. Lord Henry believes that the only way to get rid of a temptation is to yield to it.
    B. Lord Henry believes keeping a busy mind will keep the body from giving in to temptation.
    C. Lord Henry believes one must pray earnestly to God to rid oneself of temptation.
    D. Lord Henry believes honest work will keep a man from temptation.

9. What does Dorian Gray so desperately wish for that he "would give [his] soul" to have it come true?
    A. Dorian wishes for enough riches so that he will never have to work.
    B. Dorian wishes that his portrait would age while he remains young and untouched by the ugliness of life.
    C. Dorian wishes to meet and marry his soul mate.
    D. Dorian wishes that he could travel to America to study the Transcendentalists.

10. To what does Basil attribute Dorian's negative reaction to his painting?
    A. Dorian claims the painting makes him look fat.
    B. Basil believes that Dorian is just in one of his tempestuous moods and will change his mind later.
    C. Basil attributes Dorian's reaction to Lord Henry's negative influence.
    D. Lord Henry did not like the painting, so Dorian said that he did not like it either.

Assignment 2
Chapters 3-4

1. What happened to Dorian Gray's father?
    A. Dorian's father was killed in a duel.
    B. Dorian's father was a solider killed in the line of duty.
    C. Dorian's father murdered his mother and died in prison.
    D. Dorian's father abandoned his mother when she was pregnant.

2. What exercise does Lord Henry find "terribly enthralling"?
    A. Lord Henry is enthralled with intellectual pursuits.
    B. Lord Henry is enthralled by artistic exploration.
    C. Lord Henry is enthralled with the exercise of influence.
    D. Lord Henry is enthralled by brisk walks.

3. What advice does Lord Henry give the Duchess when she asks how she can become young again?
    A. Lord Henry tells her to never retire before midnight.
    B. Lord Henry tells her that the secret of being young is to repeat the follies of her youth.
    C. Lord Henry tells her to eat more oat bran.
    D. Lord Henry tells her to excersise good judgment in meeting new, younger people.

4. Who claims that Lord Henry is "extremely dangerous" yet still wishes to hear more of Henry's "philosophy of pleasure"?
    A. The Duchess
    B. Dorian Gray
    C. Mr. Erskine
    D. Basil Hallward

5. When Dorian Gray is reminded that he promised to visit Basil Hallward, where does Dorian go instead?
    A. Dorian chooses to go to the gentleman's club with Lord Henry instead of keeping his promise to visit Basil.
    B. Dorian chooses to go to the opera with Lord Henry instead of keeping his promise to visit Basil.
    C. Dorian goes home.
    D. Dorian chooses to go to the park with Lord Henry instead of keeping his promise to visit Basil.

6. Who is Victoria?
    A. Victoria is an actress in a second-rate theatre.
    B. Victoria is Dorian Gray's housekeeper.
    C. Victoria is the Duchess; it is her first name.
    D. Victoria is Lord Henry Wotton's wife.

7. With whom does Dorian fall in love?
    A. Dorian falls in love with the Duchess.
    B. Dorian falls in love with an actress, Sibyl Vane.
    C. Dorian falls in love with his housekeeper.
    D. Dorian has secretly fallen in love with Lord Henry's wife.

8. What does Lord Henry tell Dorian Gray is "the real secret of life"?
    A. The real secret of life is the search for beauty.
    B. The real secret of life is to find true love and keep it.
    C. The real secret of life is being true to one's own passions.
    D. The real secret of life is to work for one's rewards.

9. To where does Dorian want Henry and Basil to accompany him?
    A. Dorian wants them to come to the theatre to see Sibyl Vane.
    B. Dorian wants them to accompany him to visit the Duchess.
    C. Dorian wants them to come to Paris with him on holiday.
    D. Dorian wants them to join him for dinner at his home.

10. What news is in the telegram that Lord Henry receives from Dorian?
    A. Basil sends a telegram to Lord Henry informing him that Dorian has been injured in a terrible accident.
    B. Lord Henry's wife sends him a telegram informing him that she has run away with Dorian.
    C. Dorian sends a telegram to Lord Henry announcing his engagement to Sibyl Vane.
    D. Basil sends Lord Henry a telegram letting him know that Dorian has agreed to let Basil see the painting.

Assignment 3
Chapters 5-6

1. What does Mr. Issaacs do to help Sibyl and her family?
    A. He married Sibyl's mother.
    B. He advanced them 50 pounds.
    C. He helped James get out of jail.
    D. He found them a place to live.

2. By what name does Sibyl Vane know Dorian Gray?
    A. Prince Phillip
    B. Prince Charming
    C. Romeo
    D. Don Juan

3. What does Jim demand to know from his mother before he leaves for Australia?
    A. He demands to know the name of the man who is courting his sister.
    B. He demands to know why she seems to have such hatred toward him.
    C. He demands to know whether or not she was ever married to his father.
    D. He wants to know if she ever cared about him at all.

4. What threat does Jim make regarding "Prince Charming"?
    A. Jim swears that if "Prince Charming" ever hurts Sibyl, he will kill him.
    B. Jim swears that if "Prince Charming" doesn't go away and stay away, he will call the police.
    C. Jim swears that if "Prince Charming" ever hurts his mother, he will kill him.
    D. Jim swears that if "Prince Charming" dares to look at Sibyl again he will see him rot in prison.

5. What does Lord Henry say is the "real drawback to marriage"?
    A. He claims that marriage makes people unselfish and that unselfish people are colorless and lack individuality.
    B. He believes that romance cannot blossom in marriage, only in courtship.
    C. He claims that marriage makes people old, and they forget how to have fun.
    D. He believes that community property is unfair.

6. How does Dorian describe the details of his engagement to Sibyl Vane?
    A. They'd kissed backstage after one of her performances. He was so taken with Sibyl he got down on one knee and proposed before he knew what he was doing.
    B. They'd kissed backstage after one of her performances. Dorian told Sibyl that he loved her, and she said that she was unworthy to be his wife. He'd not actually proposed, but he considered himself engaged to her.
    C. Before he proposed to Sibyl, he went to Sibyl's home and asked permission from her mother and Jim.
    D. After seeing Sibyl perfom as Juliet, he immediately falls in love with her and jumps on the stage and proposes.

7. What does it mean to be "good," according to Lord Henry?
    A. To be good is to be kind and charitable to others.
    B. To be good is to be in harmony with oneself.
    C. To be good means to work hard for what you have.
    D. To be good is to do one's best to maintain youth and beauty at all costs.

8. What does Lord Henry tell Dorian Gray that he represents to the young man?
    A. Lord Henry says that he represents all the sins that Dorian has not had the courage to commit.
    B. Lord Henry says that he is Dorian's conscience sitting on his right shoulder, whispering into his ear.
    C. Lord Henry says that he is like a father-figure to Dorian.
    D. Lord Henry says that he is like Dorian's older brother.

Assignment 4
Chapters 7-8

1. When Lord Henry and Basil accompany Dorian to the theatre, what happens to make Dorian angry?
    A. That night's performance has been cancelled.
    B. They are late arriving from dinner and are not allowed to enter during the show.
    C. Sibyl is so convincing as Juliet that Dorian has become jealous of "Romeo."
    D. Sibyl's performance is terrible. Lord Henry and Basil leave during the show.

2. What explanation does Sibyl Vane offer Dorian regarding her performance?
    A. She fell ill suddenly and was not able to perform.
    B. She believes that she has given the best performance of her life now that she knows what it is to truly love.
    C. She was only doing as she had always done; Dorian's jealousy is outrageous.
    D. She no longer desires to live the lives of her characters, and she wishes to live in the real world with Dorian. She now sees the actors on the stage and not the characters she used to see. This reality has spoiled her acting.

3. What is Dorian's reaction to Sibyl's explanation for her poor performance?
    A. He apologizes for his insane jealousy and vows to trust her from then on.
    B. He says that he is no longer in love with her, and he will never see her again.
    C. He slaps her and throws her to the floor.
    D. He pulls her close and tells her nothing could ever come between them.

4. After he breaks off his relationship with Sibyl, what does Dorian notice about the painting Basil had done of him?
    A. The painting has changed, and on the face of the painting there are tears in the eyes.
    B. Someone has tampered with the painting and marred its appearance.
    C. The painting has changed, and on the face of the painting there was a touch of cruelty in the mouth.
    D. A black mold is beginning to form around the lower corners of the painting.

5. What does Dorian realize when he sees the changes in the painting?
    A. Dorian realizes how cruel he has been to Sibyl Vane, and he vows that he will make it up to her.
    B. He realizes he made the right choice not to marry Sybil.
    C. Basil must have tampered with the painting because he is angry with Dorian.
    D. He realizes he must destroy the painting before it destroys him.

6. What news is in Lord Henry's letter that Dorian does not open?
   A. The Duchess is so angry with Dorian for standing her up that she vowed to ruin his reputation.
   B. Lord Henry's note says he has learned that Sibyl Vane died in an incident at the theater.
   C. Basil Hallward is missing.
   D. Lord Henry's wife has asked for a divorce and is leaving him.

7. What choice does Dorian Gray make after Lord Henry points out how fortunate Dorian is that someone loved him so much as to kill herself for him?
   A. Dorian chooses to see the Duchess immediately to get Sibyl out of his mind.
   B. Dorian vows to never be cruel to anyone again.
   C. Dorian chooses to follow his passions and to allow the painting to bear the burden of his shame.
   D. Dorian vows to create a large memorial to Sibyl Vane.

8. What does Dorian believe would be a real pleasure to watch?
   A. He believes that it would be a real pleasure to watch the painting change while he physically remains the same.
   B. He believes that it would be a real pleasure to watch Lord Henry beg his wife not to leave him.
   C. He believes that it would be a real pleasure to see future actresses benefiting from the Sibyl Vane memorial fund.
   D. He believes that it would be a real pleasure to see the Duchess weeping and asking for forgiveness.

Assignment 5
Chapters 9-10

1. Where does Basil believe Dorian has gone after learning the news about Sibyl?
    A. He believes that Dorian has gone to see Lord Henry.
    B. He believes that Dorian has gone to the club to drink his pain away.
    C. He believes that Dorian has gone to comfort Sibyl's mother.
    D. He believes that Dorian has locked himself in his room in the dark.

2. Where does Dorian go the evening he learns of Sibyl's fate?
    A. He goes to the docks to find an opium seller in order to forget what has happened.
    B. He goes to the gentleman's club and gets drunk.
    C. He locks himself in the schoolroom in the dark.
    D. He goes to the opera with Lord Henry.

3. Who does Basil blame for the changes in Dorian?
    A. Himself
    B. Sibyl Vane
    C. Lord Henry
    D. The Duchess

4. Dorian threatens never to speak to Basil again. Why?
    A. Basil wants to tell Lord Henry to stay away from Dorian.
    B. Basil threatens to tell Dorian's grandfather about the difficulties Dorian is going through.
    C. Basil blames Dorian for Sibyl's death and wants Dorian to repent his sins.
    D. Dorian doesn't want Basil to see the painting, so he threatens never to speak to Basil again if Basil looks at it.

5. What does Basil want to do with the portrait of Dorian he painted?
    A. Basil wants to exhibit the portrait in Paris.
    B. An art collector in Paris wants to buy the portrait; he wants Dorian to sell it.
    C. He wants to buy it back from Dorian to keep for himself.
    D. He wants to destroy it because it shows too much of his own soul.

6. Who is Mrs. Leaf?
    A. She is Dorian Gray's housekeeper.
    B. She is Sibyl Vane's mother.
    C. She is Dorian's latest love interest.
    D. She is an art collector in Paris who wants to purchase Dorian's portriat.

7. Where does Dorian Gray decide to hide the painting?
    A. He hides it in the basement.
    B. He hides it in a secret room behind the drawing room wainscoting.
    C. He hides it under his bed.
    D. He hides the painting in an old schoolroom at the top of his house.

8. What does the coroner give as the official cause of Sibyl Vane's death?
    A. It was officially proclaimed an accidental death.
    B. It was officially proclaimed a murder.
    C. It was officially proclaimed death by natural causes.
    D. It was officially proclaimed a suicide.

9. What does Lord Henry send to Dorian that completely fascinates him?
    A. Lord Henry sends Dorian an invitation to join him at the Duchess's summer estate.
    B. Lord Henry sends Dorian a book about a man who kills himself for being evil.
    C. Lord Henry sends a young lady to meet Dorian.
    D. Lord Henry sends Dorian a book about a man who lived his life completely by fulfilling his senses.

10. Why is Dorian late meeting Lord Henry for dinner?
    A. Dorian is entertaining a young lady.
    B. Dorian gets so caught up in the book, he is late for dinner.
    C. Dorian is so caught up in watching his portrait change, he is late for dinner.
    D. Dorian falls asleep.

Assignment 6
Chapters 11-12

1. What becomes a huge influence over Dorian Gray's life?
    A. The book that Lord Henry gave Dorian has a huge influence over Dorian's behavior.
    B. Dorian has a secret relationship with the Duchess for several years.
    C. Dorian has a torrid affair with Lord Henry's wife.
    D. Dorian is fascinated with the way the painting changed; he just sits and watches it.

2. Why do people tend to disbelieve the rumors about Dorian Gray?
    A. His youthful beauty keeps people from believing the worst about him.
    B. He is a very dedicated worker who never neglects his duties.
    C. His donations to charity are very generous.
    D. He piously attends Mass daily.

3. What does Dorian Gray do once or twice every month during the winter, and each Wednesday evening while the season lasts?
    A. He plays Chopin with the regional orchestra.
    B. He performs with the local opera company.
    C. He goes to the theatre.
    D. He hosts lavish parties complete with extravagant food and music.

4. Which is NOT one of the activities or interests that managed to capture Dorian Gray's attention in his study of the senses?
    A. Gemstones
    B. Zoology
    C. Tapestries
    D. Catholic ritual

5. What is the Duke of Berwick's reaction when Dorian Gray is "brought by a friend into the smoking room of the Churchill"?
    A. He claps Dorian on the shoulder and introduces him to his friends.
    B. He asks Dorian if he would like to meet his daughter.
    C. He leaves when Dorian comes into the room.
    D. He picks a fist fight with Dorian.

6. To what city does Basil tell Dorian he plans to travel?
   A. Cairo
   B. Paris
   C. Amsterdam
   D. New York

7. What is it that Basil wishes to speak to Dorian about before leaving?
   A. He wants to warn him once again to stay away from Lord Henry's influence.
   B. He wants to express his admiration for Dorian.
   C. He wants to know the truth about the terrible rumors surrounding Dorian's moral character.
   D. He wants Dorian to accompany him on his trip.

8. What sort of fate have many of Dorian's acquaintances met?
   A. Most have left the country in disgrace.
   B. Those who were closest to Dorian have lost their respectable reputations in society.
   C. Many have enjoyed basking in Dorian's limelight and have increased their social standing.
   D. Many of his former friends were murdered by Dorian's worst acquaintances.

9. What does Basil claim that he would have to see before he could believe anything he's heard about Dorian's activities?
   A. Basil claims he would have to speak to Dorian's servants.
   B. Basil claims he would have to see the portrait he painted of Dorian.
   C. Basil claims he would have to read Dorian's diary.
   D. Basil claims that he would have to see Dorian's soul.

10. Where does Dorian take Basil so that the artist may see the "diary of [his] life"?
    A. Dorian takes Basil to the basement.
    B. Dorian takes Basil upstairs to the locked schoolroom.
    C. Dorian takes Basil to the secret room behind the wainscoting of the drawing room.
    D. Dorian takes Basil to his private chambers.

Assignment 7
Chapters 13-14

1. What does Basil see when he looks at the portrait he painted of Dorian Gray?
    A. Basil sees an aging man with the look of contempt in his eyes.
    B. Basil sees no changes; only Dorian can see the changes in the painting.
    C. Basil sees a bloody knife in Dorian's hand.
    D. Basil sees an aging man who has the look of a satyr.

2. What does Basil implore Dorian to do after seeing the condition of the painting?
    A. Basil begs Dorian to dispose of the painting.
    B. Basil begs Dorian to get on his knees and pray to God for forgiveness of his sins.
    C. Basil begs Dorian to burn it to send the satyr back to hell where he belongs.
    D. Basil begs Dorian to give the painting to museum.

3. What does Dorian Gray do to Basil?
    A. Dorian breaks down in tears and prays for Basil's forgiveness.
    B. Dorian tells Basil to leave and never return.
    C. Dorian viciously stabs Basil in the neck with an artist's knife.
    D. Dorian shoves Basil out of the room, and Basil accidentally falls down the stairs and breaks his neck.

4. Where does Dorian hide Basil's belongings?
    A. He hides them under his bed.
    B. He hides them in a secret compartment behind the wainscoting.
    C. He hides them in the basement behind the furnace.
    D. He hides them in the schoolroom behind the painting.

5. What does Dorian do to provide himself with an alibi regarding Basil's death?
    A. Dorian goes to the local brothel and pays one of the women to say he had been with her all night.
    B. Dorian goes outside and bangs on his door to awaken his servants. In doing so his servants will provide him with an alibi that he returned home after Basil had gone.
    C. Dorian goes to Lord Henry and asks him to provide Dorian with an alibi.
    D. Dorian goes to the club and pretends to be upset because Basil has not joined him as planned.

6. As Dorian sketches, what seems to appear in all of his drawings?
    A. His own youthful face begins to appear in all of his drawings.
    B. Basil Hallward's face begins to appear in all of his drawings.
    C. Sibyl Vane's face begins to appear in all of his drawings.
    D. The face of the portrait begins to appear in all of his drawings.

7. Who does Dorian send his servant to fetch on the morning after Basil's death?
    A. Lord Henry
    B. Adrian Singleton
    C. Basil Hallward
    D. Alan Campbell

8. In what particular field of study does Alan Campbell specialize?
    A. He specializes in medicine.
    B. He specializes in the field of science, particularly chemistry.
    C. He specalizes in covert operations.
    D. He specializes in the arts.

9. What request does Dorian Gray make of Alan Campbell?
    A. Dorian wants Alan to pose as Basil for several days around London so that people will think that Basil is still alive; meanwhile, Dorian will go to Paris, creating an alibi.
    B. Dorian asks Alan Campbell to dispose of Basil's body.
    C. Dorian wants Alan to accompany him to Paris and pretend to be Basil Hallward.
    D. Dorian wants Alan to claim responsibility for Basil's death.

10. Why does Alan Campbell agree to do as Dorian asks?
    A. Dorian pays Alan a huge amount of money to do as he asks.
    B. Dorian blackmails Alan Campbell with some deed from his past.
    C. Alan feels sorry for Dorian and wishes to help him.
    D. Alan knows that it is the only way to get Dorian Gray out of his life forever.

Assignment 8
Chapters 15-16

1. What is Dorian's mood when he attends Lady Narborough's party?
    A. He becomes loud and obnoxious after drinking far too much.
    B. He is surprisingly calm despite what had happened with Basil.
    C. He is nervous and jittery; Lord Henry remarks on his behavior.
    D. He is cantankerous and argues loudly with everyone.

2. Why does Lady Narborough seem to hate visiting her daughter and son-in-law?
    A. She is not on good terms with her daughter, and they fight constantly.
    B. She thinks that they spoil their children too much.
    C. She says that her son-in-law is not good enough for her daughter.
    D. She thinks that living in the country is too boring.

3. Whom does Lady Narbourough accuse of being "extremely wicked"?
    A. Dorian Gray
    B. Basil Hallward
    C. Her husband
    D. Lord Henry

4. What does Lord Henry ask Dorian at Lady Narbourough's party that makes Dorian nervous?
    A. Lord Henry asks if he could see the painting of Dorian just once more.
    B. Lord Henry asks Dorian where he went after leaving early the night before.
    C. Lord Henry asks if Basil is coming to the party.
    D. Lord Henry asks if Dorian has seen Basil; no one has seen him in the last 24 hours.

5. What "things that were dangerous" does Dorian believe had to be dealt with immediately upon arriving home from Lady Narborough's dinner party?
    A. Dorian has to dispose of Basil's body in another location.
    B. Dorian has to destroy all the books that have poisoned his mind over the years.
    C. Dorian buries Basil's ulster and bag to remove any evidence that Basil had been there.
    D. Dorian has to get rid of the opium stash he is hiding before it is discovered by his servants.

6. What words did Lord Henry say the first day he met Dorian that now repeatedly play through Dorian's mind?
   A. Lord Henry told Dorian that one could cure the soul by means of the senses and the senses by means of the soul.
   B. Lord Henry told Dorian that the painting truly is a reflection of Dorian's very soul.
   C. Lord Henry told Dorian that there is nothing to fear but fear itself.
   D. Lord Henry told Dorian that one could cure the soul by confessing their sins and changing their evil ways.

7. Though Dorian believes that forgiveness for his sins is impossible, what is "possible still"?
   A. Although Dorian feels he cannot be forgiven for his sins, he could still obtain forgetfulness through drugs.
   B. Although Dorian feels he cannot be forgiven for his sins, he could still obtain peace through drugs.
   C. Although Dorian feels he cannot be forgiven for his sins now, he will be able to change and in doing so be forgiven in the future.
   D. Although Dorian feels he cannot be forgiven for his sins, he could still obtain forgetfulness through drinking.

8. What former friend does Dorian Gray see at the opium house?
   A. Lord Henry
   B. James Vane
   C. Alan Campbell
   D. Adrian Singleton

9. Who is the drunken sailor who accused Dorian Gray in the street?
   A. The drunken sailor is James Vane, Sibyl Vane's older brother.
   B. The drunken sailor is a former friend of Dorian whose reputation was ruined.
   C. The drunken sailor is Basil's son.
   D. The drunken sailor is Lord Henry's cousin.

10. Why doesn't the drunken sailor shoot Dorian Gray?
    A. Lord Henry takes the gun away from the sailor before he has a change to shoot Dorian.
    B. Dorian disarms the sailor and takes him to the police.
    C. Dorian looks to young to be the man who caused Sibyl Vane to commit suicide.
    D. Dorian looks to old to be the man who caused Sibyl Vane to commit suicide.

Assignment 9
Chapters 17-18

1. With what does Lord Henry have "one quarrel"?
    A. Lord Henry's one quarrel is with Dorian.
    B. Lord Henry's one quarrel is with time.
    C. Lord Henry's one quarrel is with his wife.
    D. Lord Henry's one quarrel is with words.

2. When Gladys tells Lord Henry he values beauty far too much, what is his response?
    A. He admits it is better to be ugly than to be evil--but acknowledges it is better to be good than ugly.
    B. He thinks it is better to be beautiful than to be good--but acknowledges it is better to be good than ugly.
    C. He thinks it is better to be wealthy than to be good--but acknowledges it is better to be beautiful than ugly.
    D. He thinks it is better to be good than to be beautiful--but acknowledges it is better to be beautiful than ugly.

3. According to Lord Henry what three things, "have made . . . England what she is?"
    A. Royalty, war, and pride
    B. Faith, hope, and charity
    C. Beer, the Bible, and the seven deadly virtues
    D. Life, liberty, and the pursuit of happiness

4. What is Lord Henry's answer when the Duchess asks him to describe women?
    A. Lord Henry says women are Sphinxes without secrets.
    B. Lord Henry says women are vicious harpies.
    C. Lord Henry says women are gentle creatures.
    D. Lord Henry says women are helpless beauties.

5. What did Dorian Gray believe he had seen through the window of the conservatory?
    A. He had seen the face of Basil Hallward watching him.
    B. He had seen the face of James Vane watching him.
    C. He had seen the face of Alan Campbell watching him.
    D. He had seen the face of Sibyl Vane watching him.

6. What does Dorian Gray blame for raising "such fearful phantoms" that keep him in his house for three days?
    A. He blames Lord Henry's influence.
    B. He blames Basil Hallward.
    C. He blames his conscience.
    D. He blames James Vane.

7. What does Dorian beg Sir Geoffrey Clouston NOT to do?
    A. Dorian begs Sir Geoffrey not to shoot a hare that is jumping into the thicket.
    B. Dorian begs Sir Geoffrey not to tell what he knows about Basil's disappearance.
    C. Dorian begs Sir Geoffrey to let him shoot the rabbit that is jumping into the thicket.
    D. Dorian begs Sir Geoffrey not to shoot a fox that is jumping into the thicket.

8. What happens that Dorian Gray proclaims to be a "bad omen"?
    A. Dorian accidently shoots a man hiding in the thicket.
    B. Sir Geoffrey accidently shoots a man hiding in the thicket.
    C. Lord Henry disappears during the hunting trip.
    D. Sir Geoffrey is struck by lightning while hunting.

9. Who is the man in the thicket?
    A. James Vane
    B. Sir Geoffrey
    C. Alan Campbell
    D. Lord Henry

Assignment 10
Chapters 19-20

1. What does Dorian promise that he will do in the future?
    A. Dorian promises to be good.
    B. Dorian promises to make reparations for all the bad things he has done.
    C. Dorian promises to live each day as if it were his last.
    D. Dorian promises to leave London.

2. Who is Hetty?
    A. Hetty is a young peasant girl with whom Dorian plans to run away.
    B. Hetty is Lord Henry's niece with whom Dorian plans to run away.
    C. Hetty is Dorian's servant with whom Dorian plans to run away.
    D. Hetty is an actress who worked with Sibyl Vane, and she knows Dorian's secret.

3. Although Dorian believes he has done right by Hetty, what does Lord Henry say will be the result of Dorian's great renunciation?
    A. Lord Henry tells Dorian he is a fool and will probably be alone the rest of his life.
    B. Lord Henry tells Dorian that Hetty has told all the village girls what happened and they will all love Dorian.
    C. Lord Henry says that Dorian's jilting of Hetty has probably ruined any chance of Hetty's happiness with any other man.
    D. Lord Henry says Hetty has probably already killed herself.

4. What becomes of Alan Campbell?
    A. Alan Campbell commits suicide.
    B. Alan Campbell becomes an opium addict.
    C. Alan Campbell is arrested for his part in Basil's death.
    D. Alan Campbell leaves England to go to Australia.

5. What does Dorian tell Lord Henry that Henry immediately dismisses as impossible to believe?
    A. Dorian tells Lord Henry that he truly loves Hetty.
    B. Dorian tells Lord Henry that he is leaving England forever.
    C. Dorian tells Lord Henry that he killed Basil.
    D. Dorian tells Lord Henry that he is in love with Lord Henry's wife.

6. What does Dorian claim is "a terrible reality . . . [that] . . . can be bought, and sold, and bartered away"?
    A. The soul
    B. Conscience
    C. Love
    D. Faith

7. What is Dorian "tired of hearing . . . now"?
    A. Dorian is tired of hearing about Basil's disappearance.
    B. Dorian is tired of hearing the vicious rumors about him.
    C. Dorian is tired of Lord Henry's negative influence.
    D. Dorian is tired of hearing the sound of his own name coming from others.

8. What does Dorian believe should be the prayer of a man to a most just God instead of "Forgive us our sins"?
    A. "Give us our daily bread."
    B. "Save us from temptation."
    C. "Do as thou wilt."
    D. "Smite us for our iniquities."

9. Why does Dorian go to his portrait while thinking of Hetty Merton?
    A. Dorian goes to move the painting to another room in the house so he will never have to see it again.
    B. Dorain goes to destroy the painting.
    C. Dorian goes to pack the painting away so he can start over without the painting reminding him of his old ways.
    D. Dorian believes because he is trying to change the portrait will also change.

10. What happens to Dorian Gray?
    A. Dorian is killed by Lord Henry when Henry sees the painting.
    B. Dorian is arrested for the murder of Basil Hallward and is hanged.
    C. Dorian dies while trying to destroy the portrait.
    D. Dorian accidentally falls on the knife that he used to kill Basil.

ANSWER KEY: STUDY QUESTIONS *The Picture of Dorian Gray*

	1	2	3	4	5	6	7	8	9	10
1	C	A	B	D	C	A	D	B	D	A
2	B	C	B	D	D	A	B	D	B	A
3	A	B	C	B	C	D	C	D	C	C
4	A	C	A	C	D	B	B	B	A	A
5	D	D	A	A	A	C	B	C	B	C
6	C	D	B	B	A	B	B	A	C	A
7	C	B	B	C	D	C	D	A	A	D
8	A	A	A	A	A	B	B	D	B	D
9	B	A			D	D	B	A	A	D
10	C	C			B	B	B	C		C

VOCABULARY WORKSHEETS

VOCABULARY ASSIGNMENT 1 *The Picture of Dorian Gray*

Part I: Using Prior Knowledge and Contextual Clues

Below are the sentences in which the vocabulary words appear in the text. Read the sentence. Use any clues you can find in the sentence combined with your prior knowledge, and write what you think the underlined words mean on the lines provided.

1. In the center of the room, . . . was sitting the artist himself, Basil Hallward, whose sudden disappearance some years ago caused, at the time, such public excitement, and gave rise to so many strange <u>conjectures</u>.

2. "It is your best work, Basil, the best thing you have ever done," said Lord Henry, <u>languidly</u>.

3. . . . the two young men went out into the garden together, and <u>ensconced</u> themselves on a long bamboo seat that stood in the shade of a tall laurel bush.

4. "Well, after I had been in the room about ten minutes, talking to huge overdressed <u>dowagers</u> and tedious Academicians, I suddenly became conscious that someone was looking at me."

5. "Well, after I had been in the room about ten minutes, talking to huge overdressed dowagers and <u>tedious</u> Academicians, I suddenly became conscious that someone was looking at me."

6. "Those who are faithful know only the <u>trivial</u> side of love; it is the faithless who know love's tragedies.

7. "Oh, I am tired of sitting, and I don't want a life-sized portrait of myself," answered the lad, swinging round on the music stool, in a wilful, <u>petulant</u> manner.

8. "You are too charming to go in for <u>philanthropy</u>, Mr. Gray--far too charming."

9. --I believe that the world would gain such a fresh impulse of joy that we would forget all the <u>maladies</u> of mediaevalism, and return to the Hellenic idea--

10. "Live the wonderful life that is in you! Let nothing be lost upon you! Be always searching for new sensations. Be afraid of nothing. . . . A new <u>Hedonism</u>--that is what our century wants."

11. "The only difference between a <u>caprice</u> and a lifelong passion is that the caprice lasts a little longer."

   _____

12. He had listened to them, laughed at them, forgotten them. They had not influenced his nature. Then had come Lord Henry Wotton with his strange <u>panegyric</u> on youth, his terrible warning of its brevity.

   _____

13. The life that was to make his soul would mar his body. He would become dreadful, hideous, and <u>uncouth</u>.

   _____

14. "I beg you not to go." Dorian Gray laughed and shook his head. "I <u>entreat,</u> you."

   _____

The Picture of Dorian Gray Vocabulary Worksheet Assignment 1 Continued

Part II: Determining the Meaning -- Match the vocabulary words to their dictionary definitions.

____ 1. CONJECTURES   A. Boring, tiring, monotonous, dull

____ 2. LANGUIDLY   B. Widows who hold property derived from deceased husbands

____ 3. ENSCONCED   C. Awkward, clumsy, or unmannerly

____ 4. DOWAGERS   D. Unreasonably irritable or ill-tempered

____ 5. TEDIOUS   E. Formal or elaborate praise

____ 6. TRIVIAL   F. Judgments based on inconclusive or incomplete evidence

____ 7. PETULANT   G. Settled securely or snugly

____ 8. PHILANTHROPY   H. Undesirable conditions or disorders

____ 9. MALADIES   I. An inclination to change one's mind impulsively

____ 10. HEDONISM   J. Of very little importance or value; insignificant

____ 11. CAPRICE   K. Devotion to pleasure as a way of life

____ 12. PANEGYRIC   L. In a manner lacking in spirit or interest; listlessly; indifferently

____ 13. UNCOUTH   M. Effort or inclination to increase the well-being of humankind

____ 14. ENTREAT   N. To ask (a person) earnestly; beseech; implore

VOCABULARY ASSIGNMENT 2 *The Picture of Dorian Gray*

Part I: Using Prior Knowledge and Contextual Clues

Below are the sentences in which the vocabulary words appear in the text. Read the sentence. Use any clues you can find in the sentence combined with your prior knowledge, and write what you think the underlined words mean on the lines provided.

1. "I am told that pork-packing is the most <u>lucrative</u> profession in America, after politics."

   _____

2. "[We are lunching at] Aunt Agatha's. I have asked myself and Mr. Gray. He is her latest <u>protege</u>."

   _____

3. He invented a <u>facile</u> excuse, and having taken the vacant seat next to her, looked round to see who was there.

   _____

4. Fortunately for him she had on the other side Lord Faudel, a most intellegent middle-aged <u>mediocrity</u>, as bald as a Ministerial statement in the House of Commons, ...

   _____

5. "To get back one's youth, one has merely to repeat one's <u>follies</u>."

   _____

6. "You must come and dine with us some night. Tuesday? Are you <u>disengaged</u> Tuesday?"

   _____

7. "Some day, when you are tired of London, come down to Treadley, and <u>expound</u> to me your philosophy of pleasure over some admirable Burgundy I am fortunate enough to possess."

   _____

8. It was, in its way, a very charming room, with its high-panelled <u>wainscoting</u> of olive-stained oak, its cream-coloured frieze and ceiling of raised plaster work, ...

   _____

9. "I don't think I am likely to marry, Henry. I am too much in love. That is one of your <u>aphorisms</u>. I am putting it into practice, as I do everything that you say."

   _____

10. "I felt that this grey, monstrous London of ours, with its <u>myriads</u> of people, its sordid sinners, and its splendid sins, as you once phrased it, must have something in store for me."

    _____

11. "I felt that this grey, monstrous London of ours, with its myriads of people, its <u>sordid</u> sinners, and its splendid sins, as you once phrased it, must have something in store for me."

_____

12. "I looked out from behind the curtain, and surveyed the house. It was a <u>tawdry</u> affair, all Cupids and cornucopias, like a third-rate wedding cake."

_____

13. "You said to me once that <u>pathos</u> left you unmoved, but that beauty, mere beauty, could fill your eyes with tears."

_____

14. It was true that as one watched life in its curious <u>crucible</u> of pain and pleasure, one could not wear over one's face a mask of glass, ...

_____

15. . . . nor keep the sulphurous fumes from troubling the brain and making the imagination <u>turbid</u> with monstrous fancies and misshapen dreams.

_____

The Picture of Dorian Gray Vocabulary Worksheet Assignment 2 Continued

Part II: Determining the Meaning -- Match the vocabulary words to their dictionary definitions.

____ 1. LUCRATIVE   A. Freed from an engagement, pledge, or obligation

____ 2. PROTEGE   B. Clouded; opaque; obscured

____ 3. FACILE   C. Gaudy; showy and cheap

____ 4. MEDIOCRITY   D. Filthy or dirty; foul

____ 5. FOLLIES   E. Producing wealth; profitable

____ 6. DISENGAGED   F. Foolishness

____ 7. EXPOUND   G. A very great number of persons or things

____ 8. WAINSCOTING   H. Wood paneling for lining interior walls

____ 9. APHORISMS   I. State of being ordinary; not outstanding

____ 10. MYRIAD   J. Severe, searching test or trial

____ 11. SORDID   K. Feeling of sympathy or pity

____ 12. TAWDRY   L. Set forth or state in detail

____ 13. PATHOS   M. Easily done, performed, or used

____ 14. CRUCIBLE   N. Tersely phrased statements of truth or opinion; adages

____ 15. TURBID   O. One whose welfare is promoted by an influential person

VOCABULARY ASSIGNMENT 3 *The Picture of Dorian Gray*

Part I: Using Prior Knowledge and Contextual Clues
   Below are the sentences in which the vocabulary words appear in the text. Read the sentence. Use any clues you can find in the sentence combined with your prior knowledge, and write what you think the underlined words mean on the lines provided.

1. Thin-lipped wisdom spoke at her from a worn chair, hinted at <u>prudence</u>, quoted from that book of cowardice whose author apes the name of common sense.

   _____

2. The Wisdom altered its method and spoke of <u>espial</u> and discovery.

   _____

3. "I am afraid I may frighten the company, frighten or <u>enthrall</u> them."

   _____

4. The brightly-coloured <u>parasols</u> danced and dipped like monstrous butterflies.

   _____

5. At the Marble Arch they hailed an <u>omnibus</u>, which left them close to their shabby home in the Euston Road.

   _____

6. She consoled herself by telling Sibyl how <u>desolate</u> she felt her life would be, now that she only had one child to look after.

   _____

7. "You are quite <u>incorrigible</u>, Harry; but I don't mind. It is impossible to be angry with you."

   _____

8. "As for the lives of one's neighbours, if one wishes to be a <u>prig</u> or a Puritan, one can flaunt one's moral views about them, but they are not one's concern."

   _____

9. "Oh! I should fancy in remorse, in suffering, in . . . well, in the consciousness of <u>degradation</u>."

   _____

10. "This is," interrupted Dorian. "You must admit, Harry, that women give to men the very gold of their lives." "Possibly," he sighed, "but they <u>invariably</u> want it back in such very small change."

    _____

11. "I am so sorry, Basil, but there is only room for two in the <u>brougham</u>. You must follow us in a hansom."

    _____

12. "I am so sorry, Basil, but there is only room for two in the brougham. You must follow us in a hansom."

_____

The Picture of Dorian Gray Vocabulary Worksheet Assignment 3 Continued

Part II: Determining the Meaning -- Match the vocabulary words to their dictionary definitions.

____ 1. PRUDENCE   A. Feeling abandoned; forlorn

____ 2. ESPIAL   B. Act of watching, especially in secret

____ 3. ENTHRALL   C. Difficult or impossible to control or manage

____ 4. PARASOLS   D. Two-wheeled covered carriage with the driver's seat above and behind

____ 5. OMNIBUS   E. Vehicle carrying many passengers, used for public transport

____ 6. DESOLATE   F. Captivate or charm

____ 7. INCORRIGIBLE   G. A decline to a lower condition, quality, or level

____ 8. PRIG   H. Self-righteous person who demands pointless conformity

____ 9. DEGRADATION   I. Light, usually small umbrellas carried as protection from the sun

____ 10. INVARIABLY   J. Without variation or change, in every case

____ 11. BROUGHAM   K. Closed four-wheeled carriage with an open driver's seat in the front

____ 12. HANSOM   L. Caution with regard to practical matters; discretion

VOCABULARY ASSIGNMENT 4 *The Picture of Dorian Gray*

Part I: Using Prior Knowledge and Contextual Clues

Below are the sentences in which the vocabulary words appear in the text. Read the sentence. Use any clues you can find in the sentence combined with your prior knowledge, and write what you think the underlined words mean on the lines provided.

1. He escorted them to their box with a sort of <u>pompous</u> humility, waving his fat jeweled hands, and talking at the top of his voice.
   _____

2. She overemphasized everything that she had to say. The beautiful passage . . . was declaimed with the painful precision of a schoolgirl who had been taught to recite by some second-rate professor of <u>elocution</u>.
   _____

3. The play dragged on, and seemed <u>interminable</u>.
   _____

4. Half of the audience went out, tramping in heavy boots, and laughing. The whole thing was a <u>fiasco</u>.
   _____

5. She crouched on the floor like a wounded thing, and Dorian Gray, with his beautiful eyes, looked down at her, and his chiselled lips curled in exquisite <u>disdain</u>.
   _____

6. The air was heavy with the perfume of the flowers, and their beauty seemed to bring him an <u>anodyne</u> for his pain.
   _____

7. Under the <u>portico</u>, with its grey sun-bleached pillars, loitered a troop of draggled bareheaded girls, waiting for the auction to be over.
   _____

8. Was there some subtle <u>affinity</u> between the chemical atoms, that shaped themselves into form and colour on the canvas, and the soul that was within him?
   _____

9. He was trying to gather up the scarlet threads of life, and to weave them into a pattern; to find his way through the <u>sanguine</u> labyrinth of passion through which he was wandering.
   _____

10. "Your letter? Oh, yes, I remember. I have not read it yet, Harry. I was afraid there might be something in it that I wouldn't like. You cut life to pieces with your <u>epigrams</u>."
    _____

11. "... they hurt us by their crude violence, their absolute incoherence, their absurd want of meaning, their entire lack of style. They affect us just as vulgarity affects us."

   _____

12. "I had buried my romances in a bed of asphodel."

   _____

13. "But you must think that the lonely death in the tawdry dressing room simply as a strange lurid fragment from some Jacobean tragedy, as a wonderful scene from Webster, or Ford, or Cyril Tourneur."

   _____

14. "But suppose, Harry, I became haggard, and old, and wrinkled? What then?"

   _____

The Picture of Dorian Gray Vocabulary Worksheet Assignment 4 Continued

Part II: Determining the Meaning -- Match the vocabulary words to their dictionary definitions.

____ 1. POMPOUS   A. Anything that relieves distress or pain

____ 2. ELOCUTION   B. Natural liking for or attraction to a person, thing, idea, etc.

____ 3. INTERMINABLE   C. Concise, clever, often paradoxical statement

____ 4. FIASCO   D. Various plants of the lily family

____ 5. DISDAIN   E. Feeling of contempt for anything regarded as unworthy

____ 6. ANODYNE   F. Gruesome; horrible; revolting

____ 7. PORTICO   G. Having a gaunt, wasted, or exhausted appearance, as from prolonged suffering, exertion, or anxiety

____ 8. AFFINITY   H. Act or expression that offends good taste or propriety

____ 9. SANGUINE   I. Characterized by excessive self-esteem or exaggerated dignity

____ 10. EPIGRAM   J. Complete and humiliting failure

____ 11. VULGARITY   K. Seeming to be without an end; endless

____ 12. ASPHODEL   L. Cheerfully optimistic, hopeful, or confident

____ 13. LURID   M. Person's manner of speaking or reading aloud in public

____ 14. HAGGARD   N. Structure consisting of a roof supported by columns or piers, usually attached to a building as a porch

VOCABULARY ASSIGNMENT 5 *The Picture of Dorian Gray*

Part I: Using Prior Knowledge and Contextual Clues
Below are the sentences in which the vocabulary words appear in the text. Read the sentence. Use any clues you can find in the sentence combined with your prior knowledge, and write what you think the underlined words mean on the lines provided.

1. "He had absolutely nothing to do, almost died of ennui, and became a confirmed misanthrope."

   _____

2. "He had absolutely nothing to do, almost died of ennui, and became a confirmed misanthrope."

   _____

3. "You can't have forgotten that you assured me most solemnly that nothing in the world would induce you to send it to any exhibition."

   _____

4. "You became to me the visible incarnation of that unseen ideal whose memory haunts us artists like an exquisite dream."

   _____

5. The man was quite impassive, and waited for his orders.

   _____

6. Compared to what he saw in it of censure or rebuke, how shallow Basil's reproaches about Sibyl Vane had been!

   _____

7. Mr. Hubbard was a florid, red-whiskered little man, whose admiration for art was considerably tempered by the inveterate impecuniosity of most of the artists who dealt with him.

   _____

8. There was the huge Italian *cassone*, with its fantastically painted panels and its tarnished gilt mouldings, in which he had so often hidden himself as a boy.

   _____

9. It might escape the hideousness of sin, but the hideousness of age was in store for it. The cheeks would become hollow or flaccid.

   _____

The Picture of Dorian Gray Vocabulary Worksheet Assignment 5 Continued

Part II: Determining the Meaning -- Match the vocabulary words to their dictionary definitions.

____ 1. ENNUI A. Diminished or became tainted

____ 2. MISANTHROPE B. Without emotion; apathetic; unmoved

____ 3. INDUCE C. To bring about, produce, or cause

____ 4. INCARNATION D. Assumption of human form or nature

____ 5. IMPASSIVE E. Feeling of utter weariness and discontent resulting from satiety or lack of interest; boredom

____ 6. CENSURE F. Soft and limp; not firm; flabby

____ 7. IMPECUNIOSITY G. State of having little or no money; penniless; poor

____ 8. TARNISHED H. Criticize or reproach harshly

____ 9. FLACCID I. Hater of humankind

VOCABULARY ASSIGNMENT 6 *The Picture of Dorian Gray*

Part I: Using Prior Knowledge and Contextual Clues
Below are the sentences in which the vocabulary words appear in the text. Read the sentence. Use any clues you can find in the sentence combined with your prior knowledge, and write what you think the underlined words mean on the lines provided.

1. He procured from Paris no less than nine larger-paper copies of the first edition, and had them bound in different colours, so that they might suit his various moods.

   _____

2. Of the asceticism that deadens the senses, as of the vulgar profligacy that dulls them, it was to know nothing.

   _____

3. The orphreys were divided into panels representing scenes from the life of the Virgin, and the coronation of the Virgin was figured in coloured silks upon the hood.

   _____

4. Of such insolences and attempted slights he, of course, took no notice . . . .

   _____

5. . . . whose beauty was equalled only by his debauchery, ...

   _____

6. . . . a man passed him in the mist, walking very fast, and with the collar of his grey ulster truned up.

   _____

7. "I know the age better than you do, though you will prate about it so tediously."

   _____

The Picture of Dorian Gray Vocabulary Worksheet Assignment 6 Continued

Part II: Determining the Meaning -- Match the vocabulary words to their dictionary definitions.

____ 1. PROCURED   A. Reckless extravagance

____ 2. PROFLIGACY   B. Long, loose, heavy overcoat

____ 3. ORPHREYS   C. Obtained or gotten by care, effort, or the use of special means

____ 4. INSOLENCES   D. Contemptuously rude or impertinent behavior or speech

____ 5. DEBAUCHERY   E. Ornamental bands or borders, esp. on ecclesiastical vestments

____ 6. ULSTER   F. Excessive indulgence in sensual pleasures

____ 7. PRATE   G. Talk excessively and pointlessly; babble

VOCABULARY ASSIGNMENT 7 *The Picture of Dorian Gray*

Part I: Using Prior Knowledge and Contextual Clues

Below are the sentences in which the vocabulary words appear in the text. Read the sentence. Use any clues you can find in the sentence combined with your prior knowledge, and write what you think the underlined words mean on the lines provided.

1. It was some foul parody, some infamous, ignoble satire.

   _____

2. "There was nothing evil in it, nothing shameful. You were to me such an ideal as I shall never meet again. This is the face of a satyr . . . it has the eyes of a devil."

   _____

3. He opened the door and went out on the landing. . . . he stood bending over the balustrade, and peering down into the black seething well of darkness.

   _____

4. The man shambled down the passage in his slippers.

   _____

5. He spent a long time also over breakfast, tasting the various dishes, talking to his valet about some new liveries that he was thinking of getting made for the servants at Selby, and going through his correspondence.

   _____

6. As one read them, one seemed to be floating down the green waterways of the pink and pearl city, seated in a black gondola with silver prow and trailing curtains.

   _____

7. Time seemed to him to be crawling with feet of lead, while he by monstrous winds was being swept towards the jagged edge of some black cleft or precipice.

   _____

8. "If in some hideous dissecting-room, or fetid laboratory you found this man lying on a leaden table with red gutters scooped out in it for the blood to flow through, you would simply look upon him as an admirable subject."

   _____

The Picture of Dorian Gray Vocabulary Worksheet Assignment 7 Continued

Part II: Determining the Meaning -- Match the vocabulary words to their dictionary definitions.

____ 1. PARODY   A. Cliff with a vertical or overhanging face

____ 2. SATYR   B. An evil, lascivious man; lecher

____ 3. BALUSTRADE   C. Uniforms worn by servants

____ 4. SHAMBLED   D. Walked or went awkwardly; shuffled

____ 5. LIVERIES   E. Having an offensive odor; stinking

____ 6. GONDOLA   F. Imitate for purposes of ridicule or satire

____ 7. PRECIPICE   G. Railing at the side of a staircase or balcony

____ 8. FETID   H. Long narrow flat-bottomed boat propelled by sculling

VOCABULARY ASSIGNMENT 8 *The Picture of Dorian Gray*

Part I: Using Prior Knowledge and Contextual Clues

Below are the sentences in which the vocabulary words appear in the text. Read the sentence. Use any clues you can find in the sentence combined with your prior knowledge, and write what you think the underlined words mean on the lines provided.

1. "It is pure <u>unadulterated</u> country life. They get up early because they have so much to do, and go to bed early because they have so little to think about."

   _____

2. "Narborough wasn't perfect," cried the old lady. "If he had been, you would not have loved him, my dear lady," was the <u>rejoinder</u>.

   _____

3. Mr. Chapman began to talk in a loud voice about the situation in the House of Commons. He <u>guffawed</u> at his adversaries.

   _____

4. "I had left my latchkey at home, and my servant had to let me in. If you want any <u>corroborative</u> evidence on the subject you can ask him."

   _____

5. Innocent blood had been spilt. . . ."Ah! for that there was no <u>atonement</u>; but though forgiveness was impossible, forgetfulness was possible still, and he was determined to forget, to stamp the thing out, to crush it as one woud crush the adder that had stung one.

   _____

6. "This will do," he answered, and, having got out hastily, and given the driver the extra fare he had promised him, he walked quickly in the direction of the <u>quay</u>.

   _____

7. His meeting with Adrian Singleton had strangely moved him, and he wondered if the ruin of that young life was really to be laid at his door, as Basil Hallward had said to him such <u>infamy</u> of insult.

   _____

The Picture of Dorian Gray Vocabulary Worksheet Assignment 8 Continued

Part II: Determining the Meaning -- Match the vocabulary words to their dictionary definitions.

____ 1.   UNADULTERATED   A.   Laughed heartily and boisterously

____ 2.   REJOINDER   B.   Extremly bad reputation

____ 3.   GUFFAWED   C.   Landing place constructed along the edge of a body of water

____ 4.   CORROBORATIVE   D.   Answer to a reply; response

____ 5.   ATONEMENT   E.   Amends or reparation made for an injury or wrong

____ 6.   QUAY   F.   Serving to support or to make more certain

____ 7.   INFAMY   G.   Not mixed with impurities; without qualification

VOCABULARY ASSIGNMENT 9 *The Picture of Dorian Gray*

Part I: Using Prior Knowledge and Contextual Clues

Below are the sentences in which the vocabulary words appear in the text. Read the sentence. Use any clues you can find in the sentence combined with your prior knowledge, and write what you think the underlined words mean on the lines provided.

1. A week later Dorian Gray was sitting in the <u>conservatory</u> at Selby Royal talking to the pretty Duchess of Monmouth, ...

2. "I won't hear of it," laughed Lord Henry, sinking into a chair. From a label there is no escape! I refuse the title." "Royalties may not <u>abdicate</u>," fell as a warning from pretty lips.

3. "I shall write it in my diary tonight . . . that a burnt child loves the fire." "I am not even <u>singed</u>. My wings are untouched."

4. Sibyl Vane's brother had not come back to kill him. He had sailed away in his ship to <u>founder</u> in some winter sea.

5. He jumped from the cart, and having told the groom to take the mare home, made his way towards his guest through the withered <u>bracken</u> and rough undergrowth.

6. The keen automatic air, the brown and red lights that glimmered in the wood, the hoarse cries of the <u>beaters</u> ringing out from time to time, and the sharp snaps of the guns that followed, fascinated him, and filled him with a sense of delightful freedom.

7. "This unfortunate accident has upset me. I have a horrible <u>presentiment</u> that something of the kind may happen to me.

The Picture of Dorian Gray Vocabulary Worksheet Assignment 9 Continued

Part II: Determining the Meaning -- Match the vocabulary words to their dictionary definitions.

____ 1. CONSERVATORY   A. Greenhouse, usually attached to a dwelling

____ 2. ABDICATE   B. People who rouse or drive game from cover

____ 3. SINGED   C. Fill with water and sink

____ 4. FOUNDER   D. Feeling of evil to come

____ 5. BRACKEN   E. Renounce or relinquish a throne, right, or power

____ 6. BEATERS   F. Area overgrown with ferns and shrubs

____ 7. PRESENTIMENT   G. Burned superficially or slightly; scorched

VOCABULARY ASSIGNMENT 10 *The Picture of Dorian Gray*

Part I: Using Prior Knowledge and Contextual Clues

Below are the sentences in which the vocabulary words appear in the text. Read the sentence. Use any clues you can find in the sentence combined with your prior knowledge, and write what you think the underlined words mean on the lines provided.

1. "Civilization is not by any means an easy thing to attain to. There are only two ways by which man can reach it. One is being cultured, the other by being corrupt. Country people have no opportunity of being either, so they stagnate."

   _____

2. "I should think the novelty of the emotion must have given you a thrill of real pleasure, Dorian," interrupted Lord Henry. "But I can finish your idyll for you.

   _____

3. "My dear boy, you are really beginning to moralize. You will soon be going about like the converted, and the revivalist, waring people against all the sins of which you have grown tired."

   _____

4. "Art has no influence upon action. It annihilates the desire to act. It is superbly sterile."

   _____

5. . . . that he had been an evil influence to others, and had experienced a terrible joy in being so; and that of the lives that had crossed his own it had been the fairest and the most of promise that he had brought to shame. But was it all irretrievable?

   _____

6. Not "Forgive us our sins," but "Smite us for our iniquities," should be the prayer of man to a most just God.

   _____

7. Once, someone who had terribly loved him, had written to him a mad letter, ending with these idolatrous words: "The world is changed because you are made of ivory and gold. The curves of your lips rewrite history."

   _____

The Picture of Dorian Gray Vocabulary Worksheet Assignment 10 Continued

Part II: Determining the Meaning -- Match the vocabulary words to their dictionary definitions.

____ 1. STAGNATE A. Having excessive or blind adoration, reverence, or devotion

____ 2. IDYLL B. Unable to be recovered or regained

____ 3. REVIVALIST C. Person who promotes or holds religious revivals

____ 4. ANNIHILATES D. Simple descriptive or narrative piece in verse or prose

____ 5. IRRETRIEVABLE E. Strike down, injure, or slay

____ 6. SMITE F. Stop developing, growing, or progressing

____ 7. IDOLATROUS G. Destroys completely

VOCABULARY ANSWER KEY - *The Picture of Dorian Gray*

	1	2	3	4	5	6	7	8	9	10
1	F	E	L	I	E	C	F	G	A	F
2	L	O	B	M	I	A	B	D	E	D
3	G	M	F	K	C	E	G	A	G	C
4	B	I	I	J	D	D	D	F	C	G
5	A	F	E	E	B	F	C	E	F	B
6	J	A	A	A	H	B	H	C	B	E
7	D	L	C	N	G	G	A	B	D	A
8	M	H	H	B	A		E			
9	H	N	G	L	F					
10	K	G	J	C						
11	I	D	K	H						
12	E	C	D	D						
13	C	K		F						
14	N	J		G						
15		B								

DAILY LESSONS

LESSON ONE

Objectives
1. To become familiar with the elements of Gothic literature
2. To hear the tale *Markheim* by Robert Louis Stevenson as an introduction to the concept of the doppleganger
3. To introduce Oscar Wilde and *The Picture of Dorian Gray*
4. To preview the questions and vocabulary for Chapters 1-2
5. To read Chapters 1-2

Activity 1
Ask students to brainstorm what makes a good ghost/horror story. As students come up with ideas, make a list where all students can see it. For any of the elements they may have missed, ask leading questions so students can come up with the answers themselves.

Gothic literature contains a combination of several of these elements:

A deserted (or sparsely inhabited) castle or mansion (the bigger, the spookier) in a state of ruins or semi-ruins

Labyrinths/mazes, dark corridors, and winding stairs filled with cobwebs

Hidden tunnels/staircases, dungeons, underground passages, crypts, or catacombs

If set in a broken-down modern house, the basement or attic becomes the place of terror.

Lights mysteriously go out.

Threatening natural landscapes like rugged mountains, dark forests, or eerie moors, exhibiting stormy weather

Dark secrets surrounding some tormented soul who is left to live in isolation

Ominous omens and curses

Magic, supernatural manifestations, or the suggestion of the supernatural

A damsel in distress

The damsel's rescuer, usually a lover

Horrifying (or terrifying) events or the threat of such happenings

Activity 2
Give brief notes about the life of Oscar Wilde (see introductory materials) and discuss how certain aspects of his life might have led him to write in the Gothic Horror genre.

Activity 3
Read aloud the story "Markheim" by Robert Louis Stevenson. Since the tale is in public domain, a copy is included in these materials.

Discuss what elements of the Gothic genre can be found in this story. Be sure to include a discussion of the "doppelganger" or "evil twin" that can be found throughout literature. Some examples are "Markheim" and *Dr. Jekyll and Mr. Hyde* by Robert Louis Stevenson, "William Wilson" by Edgar Allan Poe, and Charles" by Shirley Jackson.

Activity 4
Distribute the materials students will use in this unit. Explain in detail how students are to use these materials.

Study Guides
Students should read the study guide questions for each reading assignment prior to beginning the reading to get a feeling for what events and ideas are important in the section they are about to read. After reading the section, students will (as a class or individually) answer the questions to review the important events and ideas from that section of the novel. Students should keep the study guides as study materials for the unit test. **Review the study questions for the first reading assignment (Chapters 1-2) together in class.**

Vocabulary
Prior to each reading assignment, students will do vocabulary work related to the section of the novel they are about to read. Following the completion of the novel, there will be a vocabulary review of all the words used in the vocabulary assignments. Students should keep their vocabulary work as study materials for the unit test. **Do the vocabulary worksheet for the first reading assignment (Chapters 1-2) together in class to show students how the worksheets are done.**

Reading Assignment Sheet
You need to fill in the reading assignment sheet to let students know by when their reading has to be completed. You can either copy the assignments from the sheet and place them where all students can see them or photocopy the assignment sheet and give one to each student. In either case, you should advise students to become very familiar with the reading assignments so they know what is expected of them.

Extra Activities Center
The Unit Resource Materials portion of this LitPlan contains suggestions for an in-class library of related books and articles as well as puzzles and worksheets. Make an extra activities center in your room where you will keep these materials for students to use when they finish reading or assignments early (or for extra credit).

Non-Fiction Assignment
Explain to students that they each are to read at least one non-fiction piece related to the book. Students will fill out a Non-Fiction Assignment Sheet after completing the reading to help you evaluate their reading experiences and to help the students think about and evaluate their own reading experiences.

Books
Each school has its own rules and regulations regarding student use of school books. Advise students of the procedures that are normal for your school. Preview the book looking at the cover, front-matter, etc.

Activity 5
Students should read Chapters 1-2 prior to the next class meeting. If time remains in this class, they may start this assignment.

NOTE: You may want to read aloud or play an audio recording of the first chapter to give students a good feeling for the book to get them started, depending on the level or nature of your class.

"Markheim" by Robert Louis Stevenson

"Yes," said the dealer, "our windfalls are of various kinds. Some customers are ignorant, and then I touch a dividend on my superior knowledge. Some are dishonest," and here he held up the candle, so that the light fell strongly on his visitor, "and in that case," he continued, "I profit by my virtue."

Markheim had but just entered from the daylight streets, and his eyes had not yet grown familiar with the mingled shine and darkness in the shop. At these pointed words, and before the near presence of the flame, he blinked painfully and looked aside.

The dealer chuckled. "You come to me on Christmas Day," he resumed, "when you know that I am alone in my house, put up my shutters, and make a point of refusing business. Well, you will have to pay for that; you will have to pay for my loss of time, when I should be balancing my books; you will have to pay, besides, for a kind of manner that I remark in you to-day very strongly. I am the essence of discretion, and ask no awkward questions; but when a customer cannot look me in the eye, he has to pay for it." The dealer once more chuckled; and then, changing to his usual business voice, though still with a note of irony, "You can give, as usual, a clear account of how you came into the possession of the object?" he continued. "Still your uncle's cabinet? A remarkable collector, sir!"

And the little pale, round-shouldered dealer stood almost on tiptoe, looking over the top of his gold spectacles, and nodding his head with every mark of disbelief. Markheim returned his gaze with one of infinite pity, and a touch of horror.

"This time," said he, "you are in error. I have not come to sell, but to buy. I have no curios to dispose of; my uncle's cabinet is bare to the wainscot; even were it still intact, I have done well on the Stock Exchange, and should more likely add to it than otherwise, and my errand to-day is simplicity itself. I seek a Christmas present for a lady," he continued, waxing more fluent as he struck into the speech he had prepared; "and certainly I owe you every excuse for thus disturbing you upon so small a matter. But the thing was neglected yesterday; I must produce my little compliment at dinner; and, as you very well know, a rich marriage is not a thing to be neglected."

There followed a pause, during which the dealer seemed to weigh this statement incredulously. The ticking of many clocks among the curious lumber of the shop, and the faint rushing of the cabs in a near thoroughfare, filled up the interval of silence.

"Well, sir," said the dealer, "be it so. You are an old customer after all; and if, as you say, you have the chance of a good marriage, far be it from me to be an obstacle. Here is a nice thing for a lady now," he went on, "this hand-glass--fifteenth century, warranted; comes from a good collection, too; but I reserve the name, in the interests of my customer, who was just like yourself, my dear sir, the nephew and sole heir of a remarkable collector."

The dealer, while he thus ran on in his dry and biting voice, had stooped to take the object from its place; and, as he had done so, a shock had passed through Markheim, a start both of hand and foot, a sudden leap of many tumultuous passions to the face. It passed as swiftly as it came, and left no trace beyond a certain trembling of the hand that now received the glass.

"A glass," he said hoarsely, and then paused, and repeated it more clearly. "A glass? For Christmas? Surely not?"

"And why not?" cried the dealer. "Why not a glass?"

Markheim was looking upon him with an indefinable expression. "You ask me why not?" he said.

"Why, look here--look in it--look at yourself! Do you like to see it? No! nor I--nor any man."

The little man had jumped back when Markheim had so suddenly confronted him with the mirror; but now, perceiving there was nothing worse on hand, he chuckled. "Your future lady, sir, must be pretty hard favored," said he.

"I ask you," said Markheim, "for a Christmas present, and you give me this--this damned reminder of years, and sins and follies--this hand- conscience! Did you mean it? Had you a thought in your mind? Tell me. It will be better for you if you do. Come, tell me about yourself. I hazard a guess now, that you are in secret a very charitable man."

The dealer looked closely at his companion. It was very odd, Markheim did not appear to be laughing; there was something in his face like an eager sparkle of hope, but nothing of mirth.

"What are you driving at?" the dealer asked.

"Not charitable?" returned the other, gloomily. "Not charitable; not pious; not scrupulous; unloving, unbeloved; a hand to get money, a safe to keep it. Is that all? Dear God, man, is that all?"

"I will tell you what it is," began the dealer, with some sharpness, and then broke off again into a chuckle. "But I see this is a love match of yours, and you have been drinking the lady's health."

"Ah!" cried Markheim, with a strange curiosity. "Ah, have you been in love? Tell me about that."

"I," cried the dealer. "I in love! I never had the time, nor have I the time today for all this nonsense. Will you take the glass?"

"Where is the hurry?" returned Markheim. "It is very pleasant to stand here talking; and life is so short and insecure that I would not hurry away from any pleasure--no, not even from so mild a one as this. We should rather cling, cling to what little we can get, like a man at a cliff's edge. Every second is a cliff, if you think upon it--a cliff a mile high--high enough, if we fall, to dash us out of every feature of humanity. Hence it is best to talk pleasantly. Let us talk of each other; why should we wear this mask? Let us be confidential. Who knows? we might become friends."

"I have just one word to say to you," said the dealer. "Either make your purchase, or walk out of my shop."

"True, true," said Markheim. "Enough fooling. To business. Show me something else."

The dealer stooped once more, this time to replace the glass upon the shelf, his thin blond hair falling over his eyes as he did so. Markheim moved a little nearer, with one hand in the pocket of his greatcoat; he drew himself up and filled his lungs; at the same time many different emotions were depicted together on his face--terror, horror, and resolve, fascination and a physical repulsion; and through a haggard lift of his upper lip, his teeth looked out.

"This, perhaps, may suit," observed the dealer. And then, as he began to re-arise, Markheim bounded from behind upon his victim. The long, skewer-like dagger flashed and fell. The dealer struggled like a hen, striking his temple on the shelf, and then tumbled on the floor in a heap.

Time had some score of small voices in that shop--some stately and slow as was becoming to their great age; others garrulous and hurried. All these told out the seconds in an intricate chorus of tickings. Then the passage of a lad's feet, heavily running on the pavement, broke in upon these smaller voices and startled Markheim into the consciousness of his surroundings. He looked about him awfully. The candle stood on the counter, its flame solemnly wagging in a draught; and by that inconsiderable movement the whole room was filled with noiseless bustle and kept heaving like a sea: the tall shadows nodding, the gross blots of darkness swelling and dwindling as with respiration, the faces of the portraits and the china gods changing and wavering like images in water. The inner door stood ajar, and peered into that leaguer of shadows with a long slit of daylight like a pointing finger.

From these fear-stricken rovings, Markheim's eyes returned to the body of his victim, where it lay, both humped and sprawling, incredibly small and strangely meaner than in life. In these poor, miserly clothes, in that ungainly attitude, the dealer lay like so much sawdust. Markheim had feared to see it, and, lo! it was nothing. And yet, as he gazed, this bundle of old clothes and pool of blood began to find eloquent voices. There it must lie; there was none to work the cunning hinges or direct the miracle of locomotion; there it must lie till it was found. Found! ay, and then? Then would this dead flesh lift up a cry that would ring over England, and fill the world with the echoes of pursuit. Ay, dead or not, this was still the enemy. "Time was that when the brains were out," he thought; and the first word struck into his mind. Time, now that the deed was accomplished-- time, which had closed for the victim, had become instant and momentous for the slayer.

The thought was yet in his mind, when, first one and then another, with every variety of pace and voice--one deep as the bell from a cathedral turret, another ringing on its treble notes the prelude of a waltz,--the clocks began to strike the hour of three in the afternoon.

The sudden outbreak of so many tongues in that dumb chamber staggered him. He began to bestir himself, going to and fro with the candle, beleaguered by moving shadows, and startled to the soul by chance reflections. In many rich mirrors, some of home design, some from Venice or Amsterdam, he saw his face repeated and repeated, as it were an army of spies; his own eyes met and detected him; and the sound of his own steps, lightly as they fell, vexed the surrounding quiet. And still, as he continued to fill his pockets, his mind accused him with a sickening iteration, of the thousand faults of his design. He should have chosen a more quiet hour; he should have prepared an alibi; he should not have used a knife; he should have been more cautious, and only bound and gagged the dealer, and not killed him; he should have been more bold, and killed the servant also; he should have done all things otherwise. Poignant regrets, weary, incessant toiling of the mind to change what was unchangeable, to plan what was now useless, to be the architect of the irrevocable past. Meanwhile, and behind all this activity, brute terrors, like the scurrying of rats in a deserted attic, filled the more remote chambers of his brain with riot; the hand of the constable would fall heavy on his shoulder, and his nerves would jerk like a hooked fish; or he beheld, in galloping defile, the dock, the prison, the gallows, and the black coffin.

Terror of the people in the street sat down before his mind like a besieging army. It was impossible, he thought, but that some rumor of the struggle must have reached their ears and set on edge their curiosity; and now, in all the neighboring houses, he divined them sitting motionless and with uplifted ear--solitary people, condemned to spend Christmas dwelling alone on memories of the past, and now startingly recalled from that tender exercise; happy family parties struck into silence round the table, the mother still with raised finger--every degree and age and humor, but all, by their own hearths, prying and hearkening and weaving the rope that was to hang him. Sometimes it seemed to him he could not move too softly; the clink of the tall Bohemian goblets rang out loudly like a bell; and alarmed by the bigness of the ticking, he was tempted to stop the clocks. And then, again, with a swift transition of his terrors, the very silence of the place appeared a source of peril, and a thing to strike and freeze the passer-by; and he would step more boldly, and bustle aloud among the contents of the shop, and imitate, with elaborate bravado, the movements of a busy man at ease in his own house.

But he was now so pulled about by different alarms that, while one portion of his mind was still alert and cunning, another trembled on the brink of lunacy. One hallucination in particular took a strong hold on his credulity. The neighbor hearkening with white face beside his window, the passer-by arrested by a horrible surmise on the pavement--these could at worst suspect, they could not know; through the brick walls and shuttered windows only sounds could penetrate. But here, within the house, was he alone? He knew he was; he had watched the servant set forth sweet-hearting, in her poor best, "out for the day" written in every ribbon and smile. Yes, he was alone, of course; and yet, in the bulk of empty house above him, he could surely hear a stir of delicate footing; he was surely conscious, inexplicably conscious of some presence. Ay, surely; to every room and corner of the house his imagination followed it; and now it was a faceless thing, and yet had eyes to see with; and again it was a shadow of himself; and yet again behold the image of the dead dealer, re-inspired with cunning and hatred.

At times, with a strong effort, he would glance at the open door which still seemed to repel his eyes. The house was tall, the skylight small and dirty, the day blind with fog; and the light that filtered down to the ground story was exceedingly faint, and showed dimly on the threshold of the shop. And yet, in that strip of doubtful brightness, did there not hang wavering a shadow?

Suddenly, from the street outside, a very jovial gentleman began to beat with a staff on the shop door, accompanying his blows with shouts and railleries in which the dealer was continually called upon by name. Markheim, smitten into ice, glanced at the dead man. But no! he lay quite still; he was fled away far beyond earshot of these blows and shoutings; he was sunk beneath seas of silence; and his name, which would once have caught his notice above the howling of a storm, had become an empty sound. And presently the jovial gentleman desisted from his knocking and departed.

Here was a broad hint to hurry what remained to be done, to get forth from this accusing neighborhood, to plunge into a bath of London multitudes, and to reach, on the other side of day, that haven of safety and apparent innocence--his bed. One visitor had come; at any moment another might follow and be more obstinate. To have done the deed, and yet not to reap the profit, would be too abhorrent a failure. The money--that was now Markheim's concern; and as a means to that, the keys.

He glanced over his shoulder at the open door, where the shadow was still lingering and shivering; and with no conscious repugnance of the mind, yet with a tremor of the belly, he drew near the body of his victim. The human character had quite departed. Like a suit half- stuffed with bran, the limbs lay scattered, the trunk doubled, on the floor; and yet the thing repelled him. Although so dingy and inconsiderable to the eye, he feared it might have more significance to the touch. He took the body by the shoulders, and turned it on its back. It was strangely light and supple, and the limbs, as if they had been broken, fell into the oddest postures. The face was robbed of all expression; but it was as pale as wax, and shockingly smeared with blood about one temple. That was, for Markheim, the one displeasing circumstance. It carried him back, upon the instant, to a certain fair-day in a fishers' village: a gray day, a piping wind, a crowd upon the street, the blare of brasses, the booming of drums, the nasal voice of a ballad singer; and a boy going to and fro, buried overhead in the crowd and divided between interest and fear, until, coming out upon the chief place of concourse, he beheld a booth and a great screen with pictures, dismally designed, garishly colored--Brownrigg with her apprentice, the Mannings with their murdered guest, Weare in the death-grip of Thurtell, and a score besides of famous crimes. The thing was as clear as an illusion He was once again that little boy; he was looking once again, and with the same sense of physical revolt, at these vile pictures; he was still stunned by the thumping of the drums. A bar of that day's music returned upon his memory; and at that, for the first time, a qualm came over him, a breath of nausea, a sudden weakness of the joints, which he must instantly resist and conquer.

He judged it more prudent to confront than to flee from these considerations, looking the more hardily in the dead face, bending his mind to realize the nature and greatness of his crime. So little a while ago that face had moved with every change of sentiment, that pale mouth had spoken, that body had been all on fire with governable energies; and now, and by his act, that piece of life had been arrested, as the horologist, with interjected finger, arrests the beating of the clock. So he reasoned in vain; he could rise to no more remorseful consciousness; the same heart which had shuddered before the painted effigies of crime, looked on its reality unmoved. At best, he felt a gleam of pity for one who had been endowed in vain with all those faculties that can make the world a garden of enchantment, one who had never lived and who was now dead. But of penitence, no, not a tremor.

With that, shaking himself clear of these considerations, he found the keys and advanced toward the open door of the shop. Outside, it had begun to rain smartly, and the sound of the shower upon the roof had banished silence. Like some dripping cavern, the chambers of the house were haunted by an incessant echoing, which filled the ear and mingled with the ticking of the clocks. And, as Markheim approached the door, he seemed to hear, in answer to his own cautious tread, the steps of another foot withdrawing up the stair. The shadow still palpitated loosely on the threshold. He threw a ton's weight of resolve upon his muscles, and drew back the door.

The faint, foggy daylight glimmered dimly on the bare floor and stairs; on the bright suit of armor posted, halbert in hand, upon the landing; and on the dark wood-carvings, and framed pictures that hung against the yellow panels of the wainscot. So loud was the beating of the rain through all the house that, in Markheim's ears, it began to be distinguished into many different sounds. Footsteps and sighs, the tread of regiments marching in the distance, the chink of money in the counting, and the creaking of doors held stealthily ajar, appeared to mingle with the patter of the drops upon the cupola and the gushing of the water in the pipes. The sense that he was not alone grew upon him to the verge of madness. On every side he was haunted and begirt by presences. He heard them moving in the upper chambers; from the shop, he heard the dead man getting to his legs; and as he began with a great effort to mount the stairs, feet fled quietly before him and followed stealthily behind. If he were but deaf, he thought, how tranquilly he would possess his soul! And then again, and hearkening with ever fresh attention, he blessed himself for that unresting sense which held the outposts and stood a trusty sentinel upon his life. His head turned continually on his neck; his eyes, which seemed starting from their orbits, scouted on every side, and on every side were half rewarded as with the tail of something nameless vanishing. The four and twenty steps to the first floor were four and twenty agonies.

On that first story, the doors stood ajar--three of them, like three ambushes, shaking his nerves like the throats of cannon. He could never again, he felt, be sufficiently immured and fortified from men's observing eyes; he longed to be home, girt in by walls, buried among bedclothes, and invisible to all but God. And at that thought he wondered a little, recollecting tales of other murderers and the fear they were said to entertain of heavenly avengers. It was not so, at least, with him. He feared the laws of nature, lest, in their callous and immutable procedure, they should preserve some damning evidence of his crime. He feared tenfold more, with a slavish, superstitious terror, some scission in the continuity of man's experience, some willful illegality of nature. He played a game of skill, depending on the rules, calculating consequence from cause; and what if nature, as the defeated tyrant overthrew the chessboard, should break the mould of their succession? The like had befallen

Napoleon (so writers said) when the winter changed the time of its appearance. The like might befall Markheim: the solid walls might become transparent and reveal his doings like those of bees in a glass hive; the stout planks might yield under his foot like quicksands and detain him in their clutch. Ay, and there were soberer accidents that might destroy him; if, for instance, the house should fall and imprison him beside the body of his victim, or the house next door should fly on fire, and the firemen invade him from all sides. These things he feared; and, in a sense, these things might be called the hands of God reached forth against sin. But about God himself he was at ease; his act was doubtless exceptional, but so were his excuses, which God knew; it was there, and not among men, that he felt sure of justice.

When he had got safe into the drawing room, and shut the door behind him, he was aware of a respite from alarms. The room was quite dismantled, uncarpeted besides, and strewn with packing-cases and incongruous furniture; several great pier-glasses, in which he beheld himself at various angles, like an actor on a stage; many pictures, framed and unframed, standing, with their faces to the wall; a fine Sheraton sideboard, a cabinet of marquetry, and a great old bed, with tapestry hangings. The windows opened to the floor; but by great good fortune the lower part of the shutters had been closed, and this concealed him from the neighbors. Here, then, Markheim drew in a packing case before the cabinet, and began to search among the keys. It was a long business, for there were many; and it was irksome, besides; for, after all, there might be nothing in the cabinet, and time was on the wing. But the closeness of the occupation sobered him. With the tail of his eye he saw the door--even glanced at it from time to time directly, like a besieged commander pleased to verify the good estate of his defenses. But in truth he was at peace. The rain falling in the street sounded natural and pleasant. Presently, on the other side, the notes of a piano were wakened to the music of a hymn, and the voices of many children took up the air and words. How stately, how comfortable was the melody! How fresh the youthful voices! Markheim gave ear to it smilingly, as he sorted out the keys; and his mind was thronged with answerable ideas and images: church-going children, and the pealing of the high organ; children afield, bathers by the brookside, ramblers on the brambly common, kite-flyers in the windy and cloud-navigated sky; and then, at another cadence of the hymn, back again to church, and the somnolence of summer Sundays, and the high genteel voice of the parson (which he smiled a little to recall) and the painted Jacobean tombs, and the dim lettering of the Ten Commandments in the chancel.

And as he sat thus, at once busy and absent, he was startled to his feet. A flash of ice, a flash of fire, a bursting gush of blood, went over him, and then he stood transfixed and thrilling. A step mounted the stair slowly and steadily, and presently a hand was laid upon the knob, and the lock clicked, and the door opened.

Fear held Markheim in a vice. What to expect he knew not--whether the dead man walking, or the official ministers of human justice, or some chance witness blindly stumbling in to consign him to the gallows. But when a face was thrust into the aperture, glanced round the room, looked at him, nodded and smiled as if in friendly recognition, and then withdrew again, and the door closed behind it, his fear broke loose from his control in a hoarse cry. At the sound of this the visitant returned.

"Did you call me?" he asked, pleasantly, and with that he entered the room and closed the door behind him.

Markheim stood and gazed at him with all his eyes. Perhaps there was a film upon his sight, but the outlines of the new comer seemed to change and waver like those of the idols in the wavering candle-light of the shop; and at times he thought he knew him; and at times he thought he bore a likeness to himself; and always, like a lump of living terror, there lay in his bosom the conviction that this thing was not of the earth and not of God.

And yet the creature had a strange air of the commonplace, as he stood looking on Markheim with a smile; and when he added, "You are looking for the money, I believe?" it was in the tones of everyday politeness.

Markheim made no answer.

"I should warn you," resumed the other, "that the maid has left her sweetheart earlier than usual and will soon be here. If Mr. Markheim be found in this house, I need not describe to him the consequences."

"You know me?" cried the murderer.

The visitor smiled. "You have long been a favorite of mine," he said; "and I have long observed and often sought to help you."

"What are you?" cried Markheim; "the devil?"

"What I may be," returned the other, "cannot affect the service I propose to render you."

"It can," cried Markheim; "it does! Be helped by you? No, never; not by you! You do not know me yet; thank God, you do not know me!"

"I know you," replied the visitant, with a sort of kind severity or rather firmness. "I know you to the soul."

"Know me!" cried Markheim. "Who can do so? My life is but a travesty and slander on myself. I have lived to belie my nature. All men do; all men are better than this disguise that grows about and stifles them. You see each dragged away by life, like one whom bravos have seized and muffled in a cloak. If they had their own control--if you could see their faces, they would be altogether different, they would shine out for heroes and saints! I am worse than most; myself is more overlaid; my excuse is known to me and God. But, had I the time, I could disclose myself."

"To me?" inquired the visitant.

"To you before all," returned the murderer. "I supposed you were intelligent. I thought--since you exist--you would prove a reader of the heart. And yet you would propose to judge me by my acts! Think of it--my acts! I was born and I have lived in a land of giants; giants have dragged me by the wrists since I was born out of my mother--the giants of circumstance. And you would judge me by my acts! But can you not look within? Can you not understand that evil is hateful to me? Can you not see within me the clear writing of conscience, never blurred by any willful sophistry, although too often disregarded? Can you not read me for a thing that surely must be common as humanity--the unwilling sinner?"

"All this is very feelingly expressed," was the reply, "but it regards me not. These points of consistency are beyond my province, and I care not in the least by what compulsion you may have been dragged away, so as you are but carried in the right direction. But time flies; the servant delays, looking in the faces of the crowd and at the pictures on the hoardings, but still she keeps moving nearer; and remember, it is as if the gallows itself was striding towards you through the Christmas streets! Shall I help you--I, who know all? Shall I tell you where to find the money?"

"For what price?" asked Markheim.

"I offer you the service for a Christmas gift," returned the other.

Markheim could not refrain from smiling with a kind of bitter triumph. "No," said he, "I will take nothing at your hands; if I were dying of thirst, and it was your hand that put the pitcher to my lips, I should find the courage to refuse. It may be credulous, but I will do nothing to commit myself to evil."

"I have no objection to a death-bed repentance," observed the visitant.

"Because you disbelieve their efficacy!" Markheim cried.

"I do not say so," returned the other; "but I look on these things from a different side, and when the life is done my interest falls. The man has lived to serve me, to spread black looks under color of religion, or to sow tares in the wheat-field, as you do, in a course of weak compliance with desire. Now that he draws so near to his deliverance, he can add but one act of service: to repent, to die smiling, and thus to build up in confidence and hope the more timorous of my surviving followers. I am not so hard a master. Try me; accept my help. Please yourself in life as you have done hitherto; please yourself more amply, spread your elbows at the board; and when the night begins to fall and the curtains to be drawn, I tell you, for your greater comfort, that you will find it even easy to compound your quarrel with your conscience, and to make a truckling peace with God. I came but now from such a death-bed, and the room was full of sincere mourners, listening to the man's last words; and when I looked into that face, which had been set as a flint against mercy, I found it smiling with hope."

"And do you, then, suppose me such a creature?" asked Markheim. "Do you think I have no more generous aspirations than to sin and sin and sin and at last sneak into heaven? My heart rises at the thought. Is this, then, your experience of mankind? or is it because you find me with red hands that you presume such baseness? And is this crime of murder indeed so impious as to dry up the very springs of good?"

"Murder is to me no special category," replied the other. "All sins are murder, even as all life is war. I behold your race, like starving mariners on a raft, plucking crusts out of the hands of famine and feeding on each other's lives. I follow sins beyond the moment of their acting; I find in all that the last consequence is death, and to my eyes, the pretty maid who thwarts her mother with such taking graces on a question of a ball, drips no less visibly with human gore than such a murderer as yourself. Do I say that I follow sins? I follow virtues also. They differ not by the thickness of a nail; they are both scythes for the reaping angel of Death. Evil, for which I live, consists not in action but in character. The bad man is dear to me, not the bad act, whose fruits, if we could follow them far enough down the hurtling cataract of the ages, might yet be found more blessed than those of the rarest virtues. And it is not because you have killed a dealer, but because you are Markheim, that I offer to forward your escape."

"I will lay my heart open to you," answered Markheim. "This crime on which you find me is my last. On my way to it I have learned many lessons; itself is a lesson--a momentous lesson. Hitherto I have been driven with revolt to what I would not; I was a bond-slave to poverty, driven and scourged. There are robust virtues that can stand in these temptations; mine was not so; I had a thirst of pleasure. But today, and out of this deed, I pluck both warning and riches--both the power and a fresh resolve to be myself. I become in all things a free actor in the world; I begin to see myself all changed, these hands the agents of good, this heart at peace. Something comes over me out of the past--something of what I have dreamed on Sabbath evenings to the sound of the church organ, of what I forecast when I shed tears over noble books, or talked, an innocent child, with my mother. There lies my life; I have wandered a few years, but now I see once more my city of destination."

"You are to use this money on the Stock Exchange, I think?" remarked the visitor; "and there, if I mistake not, you have already lost some thousands?"

"Ah," said Markheim, "but this time I have a sure thing."

"This time, again, you will lose," replied the visitor quietly.

"Ah, but I keep back the half!" cried Markheim.

"That also you will lose," said the other.

The sweat started upon Markheim's brow. "Well then, what matter?" he exclaimed. "Say it be lost, say I am plunged again in poverty, shall one part of me, and that the worse, continue until the end to override the better? Evil and good run strong in me, hailing me both ways. I do not love the one thing; I love all. I can conceive great deeds, renunciations, martyrdoms; and though I be fallen to such a crime as murder, pity is no stranger to my thoughts. I pity the poor; who knows their trials better than myself? I pity and help them. I prize love; I love honest laughter; there is no good thing nor true thing on earth but I love it from my heart. And are my vices only to direct my life, and my virtues to lie without effect, like some passive lumber of the mind? Not so; good, also, is a spring of acts."

But the visitant raised his finger. "For six and thirty years that you have been in this world," said he, "through many changes of fortune and varieties of humor, I have watched you steadily fall. Fifteen years ago you would have started at a theft. Three years back you would have blenched at the name of murder. Is there any crime, is there any cruelty or meanness, from which you still recoil? Five years from now I shall detect you in the fact! Downward, downward, lies your way; nor can anything but death avail to stop you."

"It is true," Markheim said huskily, "I have in some degree complied with evil. But it is so with all; the very saints, in the mere exercise of living, grow less dainty, and take on the tone of their surroundings."

"I will propound to you one simple question," said the other; "and as you answer I shall read to you your moral horoscope. You have grown in many things more lax; possibly you do right to be so; and at any account, it is the same with all men. But granting that, are you in any one particular, however trifling, more difficult to please with your own conduct, or do you go in all things with a looser rein?"

"In any one?" repeated Markheim, with an anguish of consideration. "No," he added, with despair; "in none! I have gone down in all."

"Then," said the visitor, "content yourself with what you are, for you will never change; and the words of your part on this stage are irrevocably written down."

Markheim stood for a long while silent, and, indeed, it was the visitor who first broke the silence. "That being so," he said, "shall I show you the money?"

"And grace?" cried Markheim.

"Have you not tried it?" returned the other. "Two or three years ago did I not see you on the platform of revival meetings, and was not your voice the loudest in the hymn?"

"It is true," said Markheim; "and I see clearly what remains for me by way of duty. I thank you for these lessons from my soul; my eyes are opened, and I behold myself at last for what I am."

At this moment, the sharp note of the door-bell rang through the house; and the visitant, as though this were some concerted signal for which he had been waiting, changed at once in his demeanor.

"The maid!" he cried. "She has returned, as I forewarned you, and there is now before you one more difficult passage. Her master, you must say, is ill; you must let her in, with an assured but rather serious countenance; no smiles, no overacting, and I promise you success! Once the girl within, and the door closed, the same dexterity that has already rid you of the dealer will relieve you of this last danger in your path. Thenceforward you have the whole evening--the whole night, if needful--to ransack the treasures of the house and to make good your safety. This is help that comes to you with the mask of danger. Up!" he cried; "up, friend. Your life hangs trembling in the scales; up, and act!"

Markheim steadily regarded his counselor. "If I be condemned to evil acts," he said, "there is still one door of freedom open: I can cease from action. If my life be an ill thing, I can lay it down. Though I be, as you say truly, at the beck of every small temptation, I can yet, by one decisive gesture, place myself beyond the reach of all. My love of good is damned to barrenness; it may, and let it be! But I have still my hatred of evil; and from that, to your galling disappointment, you shall see that I can draw both energy and courage."

The features of the visitor began to undergo a wonderful and lovely change: they brightened and softened with a tender triumph, and, even as they brightened, faded and dislimned. But Markheim did not pause to watch or understand the transformation. He opened the door and went downstairs very slowly, thinking to himself. His past went soberly before him; he beheld it as it was, ugly and strenuous like a dream, random as chance-medley--a scene of defeat. Life, as he thus reviewed it, tempted him no longer; but on the further side he perceived a quiet haven for his bark. He paused in the passage, and looked into the shop, where the candle still burned by the dead body. It was strangely silent. Thoughts of the dealer swarmed into his mind, as he stood gazing. And then the bell once more broke out into impatient clamor.

He confronted the maid upon the threshold with something like a smile.

"You had better go for the police," said he; "I have killed your master."

LESSON TWO

Objectives
1. To review the main events, ideas, and vocabulary for Chapters 1-2
2. To demonstrate reading comprehension through responses to study questions
3. To read non-fiction articles relating to public scandals involving the rich and famous and relate them to *The Picture of Dorian Gray*
4. To practice research skills
5. To preview the study questions and vocabulary for Chapters 3-4
6. To read Chapters 3-4

Activity 1
Give students a few minutes to formulate answers to the study guide questions from Chapters 1-2 then discuss the answers to the questions in detail. Write the answers on the board so students can have the correct answers for study purposes.

NOTE: It is good practice in public speaking and leadership skills for individual students to take charge of leading the discussions of the study questions. Perhaps a different student could go to the front of the class and lead the discussion each day that the study questions are discussed in this unit. Of course, you should guide the discussion when appropriate and try to fill in any gaps students may leave. The study questions could really be handled in a number of different ways, including in small groups with group reports following. Occasionally you may want to use the multiple choice questions as quizzes to check students' reading comprehension. As a short review now and then, students could pair up for the first (or last, if you have time left at the end of a class period) few minutes of class to quiz each other from the study questions. Mix up the methods of reviewing the materials and checking comprehension throughout the unit so students don't get bored just answering the questions the same way each day. Variety in methods will also help address the different learning styles of your students.

From now on in this unit the directions will simply say, "Discuss the answers to the study questions as previously directed." You will choose the method of preparation and discussion each day based on what best suits you and your class.

Activity 2
Discuss or post the answers to the vocabulary worksheet for Chapters 1-2.

Activity 3
Give students the Non-Fiction Assignment Sheet (if you haven't already) and discuss the assignment in detail. Each student will complete a non-fiction sheet based on the particular articles relating to scandals involving the rich and famous he/she finds in the library. Encourage each student to choose a different topic; there are enough stories in the news to go around!

Students will report their findings in Lesson Six (a lesson on "dandyism") and relate their findings to *The Picture of Dorian Gray*.

Your criteria for evaluating this report will vary depending on the level of your students. You may wish for students to give a complete report without using notes of any kind, you may want students to read directly from a written report, or you may want to do something in between these two extremes. Just make students aware of your criteria in ample time for them to prepare their reports.

Activity 4
Prior to reading Chapters 3-4, students should preview the study questions and do the vocabulary worksheet. This pre-reading work as well as the reading of this section of the book should be completed prior to the next class meeting. If time remains in the class period, students my begin this assignment.

NOTE: Previewing the study questions, doing the vocabulary work, and reading the noted chapter/chapters will hereafter be referred to as doing the pre-reading work and reading.

NON-FICTION ASSIGNMENT *The Picture of Dorian Gray*

In Oscar Wilde's novel, young Dorian Gray is one of the wealthy aristocrats of nineteenth century England; he does not have to work for a living. As a result, Dorian has a lot of free time on his hands and eventually devotes his time to participating in scandalous activities. However, Dorian is clever enough not to get caught directly, so his involvement in these exploits results in mere rumors. His acquaintances, unfortunately, are not as clever--and as a result land themselves in the midst of public scandals.

Your assignment is to research modern scandals involving the rich and famous who seem to have more money and time than they know what to do with and subsequently end up in one scandalous story after another. Each student must research a different scandal; do not duplicate topics with others in the class. Check the topic list before moving forward with your assignment. You will also need to create a presentation about your topic to share with the class.

NON-FICTION ASSIGNMENT SHEET
(To be completed after reading the required non-fiction article)

Name _____ Date _____

Title of Non-fiction Read_____

Written By _____ Publication Date _____

I. Factual Summary: Write a short summary of the piece you read.

II. Vocabulary
    1. With which vocabulary words in the piece did you encounter some degree of difficulty?

    2. How did you resolve your lack of understanding with these words?

III. Interpretation: What was the main point the author wanted you to get from reading his work?

IV. Criticism
    1. With which points of the piece did you agree or find easy to accept? Why?

    2. With which points of the piece did you disagree or find difficult to believe? Why?

V. Personal Response: What do you think about this piece? OR How does this piece influence your ideas/thinking?

LESSON THREE

Objectives
1. To review the main events, ideas, and vocabulary for Chapters 3-4
2. To evaluate students' reading comprehension through a quiz
3. To demonstrate critical thinking skills through connecting the tale of King Midas to the novel
4. To preview the study questions and vocabulary for Chapters 5-6
5. To read Chapters 5-6

Activity 1
Discuss the answers to the study questions for Chapters 3-4 as previously directed.

Activity 2
Discuss or post the answers to the vocabulary worksheet for Chapters 3-4 so students have the correct answers for study purposes.

Activity 3
Distribute the quizzes for Chapters 1-4 and give students ample time to complete them. Collect the completed quizzes for grading or grade them orally together as a class.

Activity 4
Ask students to think carefully about the following question: If you could have just one wish, what would it be? Warn them to be careful of what they wish because it might come true! Allow students a few minutes to write a jorunal entry about what they would wish--and why they would wish for it. What would they do as a result of receiving the granted wish? How might it improve their lives? What possible negative results might they foresee?

Read the following story about King Midas. After the story, ask students to share their wishes and possible problems with the wishes.

Have students re-read the section of the novel about Dorian Gray's wish that his portrait would age instead of him. How might Dorian's wish relate to King Midas's? What about students' own wishes?

Activity 5
Tell students to do the pre-reading work and reading for Chapters 5-6 prior to the next class meeting. If time remains in this class period, students may start on this assignment.

KING MIDAS

King Midas was a very kind man who ruled his kingdom fairly, but he was not one to think very deeply about what he said. One day, while walking in his garden, he saw an elderly satyr asleep in the flowers. Taking pity on the old fellow, King Midas let him go without punishment. When the god Dionysus heard about it, he rewarded King Midas by granting him one wish. The king thought for only a second and then said, "I wish for everything I touch to turn to gold." And so it was.

The beautiful flowers in his garden turned toward the sun for light, but when Midas approached and touched them, they stood rigid and gold. The king grew hungry and thin, for each time he tried to eat, he found that his meal turned to gold. His lovely daughter, at his loving touch, turned hard and fast to gold. His water, his bed, his clothes, his friends, and eventually the whole palace turned to gold.

King Midas saw that soon his whole kingdom would turn to gold unless he did something right away. He asked Dionysus to turn everything back to the way it had been and take back his golden touch. Because the king was ashamed and very sad, Dionysus took pity on him and granted his request. Instantly, King Midas was poorer than he had been, but richer, he felt, in the things that really matter.

The Picture of Dorian Gray QUIZ CHAPTERS 1-4

I. Multiple Choice

1. With whom does Dorian fall in love?
   A. Dorian has secretly fallen in love with Lord Henry's wife.
   B. Dorian falls in love with the Duchess.
   C. Dorian falls in love with his housekeeper.
   D. Dorian falls in love with an actress, Sibyl Vane.

2. What does Lord Henry tell Dorian Gray is "the real secret of life"?
   A. The real secret of life is the search for beauty.
   B. The real secret of life is being true to one's own passions.
   C. The real secret of life is to work for one's rewards.
   D. The real secret of life is to find true love and keep it.

3. Who is Basil Hallward?
   A. He is a young man of great beauty.
   B. He is a London artist who paints the portrait of young Dorian Gray.
   C. He is a wealthy landlord.
   D. He is the chief constable in London.

4. What reason does Basil give for not wanting to exhibit his painting of Dorian Gray?
   A. He hates the painting and does not want anyone to see it.
   B. He is afraid others will laugh at the painting's quality.
   C. He painted it for Dorian, and it is not his to exhibit.
   D. He feels that he has put too much of his own self into the painting, and it reveals the secrets of his soul.

5. Why doesn't Basil want to introduce Lord Henry to Dorian Gray?
   A. Lord Henry is an evil old man who would ruin Dorian's reputation.
   B. Lord Henry is a known thief, and Basil wants to protect Dorian from involvement.
   C. Basil is afraid for Dorian's safety.
   D. Basil is afraid that Lord Henry will be a negative influence on the young Dorian.

6. What does Lord Henry claim is "the aim of life"?
   A. Lord Henry claims that good deeds are the "aim of life."
   B. Lord Henry claims the pursuit of happiness is the "aim of life."
   C. Lord Henry claims that truth is the "aim of life."
   D. Lord Henry claims that self-development is the "aim of life."

7. What does Dorian Gray so desperately wish for that he "would give [his] soul" to have it come true?
   A. Dorian wishes that his portrait would age while he remains young and untouched by the ugliness of life.
   B. Dorian wishes to meet and marry his soul mate.
   C. Dorian wishes that he could travel to America to study the Transcendentalists.
   D. Dorian wishes for enough riches so that he will never have to work.

8. To what does Basil attribute Dorian's negative reaction to his painting?
   A. Basil attributes Dorian's reaction to Lord Henry's negative influence.
   B. Dorian claims the painting makes him look fat.
   C. Basil believes that Dorian is just in one of his tempestuous moods and will change his mind later.
   D. Lord Henry did not like the painting, so Dorian said that he did not like it either.

9. Who is Victoria?
   A. Victoria is Lord Henry Wotton's wife.
   B. Victoria is the Duchess; it is her first name.
   C. Victoria is Dorian Gray's housekeeper.
   D. Victoria is an actress in a second-rate theatre.

10. What news is in the telegram that Lord Henry receives from Dorian?
    A. Lord Henry's wife sends him a telegram informing him that she has run away with Dorian.
    B. Basil sends a telegram to Lord Henry informing him that Dorian has been injured in a terrible accident.
    C. Basil sends Lord Henry a telegram letting him know that Dorian has agreed to let Basil see the painting.
    D. Dorian sends a telegram to Lord Henry announcing his engagement to Sibyl Vane.

The Picture of Dorian Gray QUIZ CHAPTERS 1-4 Answer Key

I. Multiple Choice

D 1. With whom does Dorian fall in love?
- A. Dorian has secretly fallen in love with Lord Henry's wife.
- B. Dorian falls in love with the Duchess.
- C. Dorian falls in love with his housekeeper.
- D. Dorian falls in love with an actress, Sibyl Vane.

A 2. What does Lord Henry tell Dorian Gray is "the real secret of life"?
- A. The real secret of life is the search for beauty.
- B. The real secret of life is being true to one's own passions.
- C. The real secret of life is to work for one's rewards.
- D. The real secret of life is to find true love and keep it.

B 3. Who is Basil Hallward?
- A. He is a young man of great beauty.
- B. He is a London artist who paints the portrait of young Dorian Gray.
- C. He is a wealthy landlord.
- D. He is the chief constable in London.

D 4. What reason does Basil give for not wanting to exhibit his painting of Dorian Gray?
- A. He hates the painting and does not want anyone to see it.
- B. He is afraid others will laugh at the painting's quality.
- C. He painted it for Dorian, and it is not his to exhibit.
- D. He feels that he has put too much of his own self into the painting, and it reveals the secrets of his soul.

D 5. Why doesn't Basil want to introduce Lord Henry to Dorian Gray?
- A. Lord Henry is an evil old man who would ruin Dorian's reputation.
- B. Lord Henry is a known thief, and Basil wants to protect Dorian from involvement.
- C. Basil is afraid for Dorian's safety.
- D. Basil is afraid that Lord Henry will be a negative influence on the young Dorian.

D 6. What does Lord Henry claim is "the aim of life"?
   A. Lord Henry claims that good deeds are the "aim of life."
   B. Lord Henry claims the pursuit of happiness is the "aim of life."
   C. Lord Henry claims that truth is the "aim of life."
   D. Lord Henry claims that self-development is the "aim of life."

A 7. What does Dorian Gray so desperately wish for that he "would give [his] soul" to have it come true?
   A. Dorian wishes that his portrait would age while he remains young and untouched by the ugliness of life.
   B. Dorian wishes to meet and marry his soul mate.
   C. Dorian wishes that he could travel to America to study the Transcendentalists.
   D. Dorian wishes for enough riches so that he will never have to work.

A 8. To what does Basil attribute Dorian's negative reaction to his painting?
   A. Basil attributes Dorian's reaction to Lord Henry's negative influence.
   B. Dorian claims the painting makes him look fat.
   C. Basil believes that Dorian is just in one of his tempestuous moods and will change his mind later.
   D. Lord Henry did not like the painting, so Dorian said that he did not like it either.

A 9. Who is Victoria?
   A. Victoria is Lord Henry Wotton's wife.
   B. Victoria is the Duchess; it is her first name.
   C. Victoria is Dorian Gray's housekeeper.
   D. Victoria is an actress in a second-rate theatre.

D 10. What news is in the telegram that Lord Henry receives from Dorian?
   A. Lord Henry's wife sends him a telegram informing him that she has run away with Dorian.
   B. Basil sends a telegram to Lord Henry informing him that Dorian has been injured in a terrible accident.
   C. Basil sends Lord Henry a telegram letting him know that Dorian has agreed to let Basil see the painting.
   D. Dorian sends a telegram to Lord Henry announcing his engagement to Sibyl Vane.

LESSON FOUR

Objectives

1. To review the main events, ideas, and vocabulary for Chapters 5-6
2. To demonstrate an understanding of characterization through the creation of character posters
3. To demonstrate understanding of the difference between a physical characteristic and a character trait
4. To improve cooperative learning skills through group work
5. To practice public speaking through presentations
6. To practice note-taking skills
7. To preview the study questions and vocabulary for Chapters 7-8
8. To read Chapters 7-8

Activity 1
Discuss the answers to the study questions for Chapters 5-6 as previously directed.

Activity 2
Discuss or post the answers to the vocabulary worksheet for Chapters 5-6 so students have the correct answers for study purposes.

Activity 3
Divide students into 6 groups. Assign each group one of the following characters: Dorian Gray, Basil Hallwoard, Lord Henry Wotton, Sibyl Vane, James Vane, and Sibyl's mother.

Give each group a large sheet of construction paper on which they will create a character poster. On each poster the groups must provide the following:

The character's name

A labeled picture of the character based on the physical description given in the text (Labels should contain page numbers as evidence.)

A list of at least three positive character traits with supporting evidence and corresponding page numbers for each

A list of at least three negative character traits with supporting evidence and corresponding page numbers for each

Give students ample time to complete their projects, and then have each group present its poster to the class while the rest of the class takes notes about all characters.

Activity 4
Tell students to do the pre-reading work and reading for Chapters 7-8 prior to the next class. If time remains in this class period, students may begin working on this assignment.

LESSON FIVE

Objectives
1. To review the main events, ideas, and vocabulary for Chapters 7-8
2. To demonstrate reading comprehension through taking a quiz
3. To practice and evaluate oral reading skills
4. To preview the study questions and vocabulary for Chapters 9-10
5. To read Chapter 9-10

Activity 1
Discuss the answers to the study questions for Chapters 7-8 as previously directed.

Preview the study questions for Chapters 9-10 together orally in class while students have their study guides out.

Activity 2
Discuss or post the answers to the vocabulary worksheet for Chapters 7-8 so students have the correct answers for study purposes.

Complete the vocabulary work for Chapters 9-10 orally together in class.

Activity 3
Distribute the quizzes for Chapters 5-8. Give students ample time to complete the quizzes, then collect them for grading or grade them orally in class.

Activity 4
Read Chapters 9-10 of *The Picture of Dorian Gray* orally in class. You probably know the best way to get readers in your class: pick students at random, ask for volunteers, or use whatever method works best for your group.

Your group may need to have passages assigned prior to class to give them a chance to practice the reading.

If you have not completed an oral reading evaluation for your students this marking period, this would be a good opportunity to do so. An Oral Reading Evaluation Form is included with this unit for your convenience.

The Picture of Dorian Gray QUIZ CHAPTERS 5-8

I. Multiple Choice

1. By what name does Sibyl Vane know Dorian Gray?
    A. Prince Charming
    B. Prince Phillip
    C. Romeo
    D. Don Juan

2. What does Jim demand to know from his mother before he leaves for Australia?
    A. He wants to know if she ever cared about him at all.
    B. He demands to know why she seems to have such hatred toward him.
    C. He demands to know whether or not she was ever married to his father.
    D. He demands to know the name of the man who is courting his sister.

3. What does it mean to be "good," according to Lord Henry?
    A. To be good is to be in harmony with oneself.
    B. To be good is to be kind and charitable to others.
    C. To be good is to do one's best to maintain youth and beauty at all costs.
    D. To be good means to work hard for what you have.

4. When Lord Henry and Basil accompany Dorian to the theatre, what happens to make Dorian angry?
    A. They are late arriving from dinner and are not allowed to enter during the show.
    B. That night's performance has been cancelled.
    C. Sibyl's performance is terrible. Lord Henry and Basil leave during the show.
    D. Sibyl is so convincing as Juliet that Dorian has become jealous of "Romeo."

5. What explanation does Sibyl Vane offer Dorian regarding her performance?
    A. She believes that she has given the best performance of her life now that she knows what it is to truly love.
    B. She no longer desires to live the lives of her characters, and she wishes to live in the real world with Dorian. She now sees the actors on the stage and not the characters she used to see. This reality has spoiled her acting.
    C. She fell ill suddenly and was not able to perform.
    D. She was only doing as she had always done; Dorian's jealousy is outrageous.

6. What is Dorian's reaction to Sibyl's explanation for her poor performance?
    A. He slaps her and throws her to the floor.
    B. He apologizes for his insane jealousy and vows to trust her from then on.
    C. He pulls her close and tells her nothing could ever come between them.
    D. He says that he is no longer in love with her, and he will never see her again.

7. What does Dorian realize when he sees the changes in the painting?
    A. He realizes he made the right choice not to marry Sybil.
    B. Dorian realizes how cruel he has been to Sibyl Vane, and he vows that he will make it up to her.
    C. He realizes he must destroy the painting before it destroys him.
    D. Basil must have tampered with the painting because he is angry with Dorian.

8. What news is in Lord Henry's letter that Dorian does not open?
    A. Lord Henry's note says he has learned that Sibyl Vane died in an incident at the theater.
    B. Lord Henry's wife has asked for a divorce and is leaving him.
    C. Basil Hallward is missing.
    D. The Duchess is so angry with Dorian for standing her up that she vowed to ruin his reputation.

9. What choice does Dorian Gray make after Lord Henry points out how fortunate Dorian is that someone loved him so much as to kill herself for him?
    A. Dorian chooses to follow his passions and to allow the painting to bear the burden of his shame.
    B. Dorian chooses to see the Duchess immediately to get Sibyl out of his mind.
    C. Dorian vows to create a large memorial to Sibyl Vane.
    D. Dorian vows to never be cruel to anyone again.

10. What does Dorian believe would be a real pleasure to watch?
    A. He believes that it would be a real pleasure to watch Lord Henry beg his wife not to leave him.
    B. He believes that it would be a real pleasure to see the Duchess weeping and asking for forgiveness.
    C. He believes that it would be a real pleasure to watch the painting change while he physically remains the same.
    D. He believes that it would be a real pleasure to see future actresses benefiting from the Sibyl Vane memorial fund.

The Picture of Dorian Gray QUIZ CHAPTERS 5-8 Answer Key

I. Multiple Choice

A 1. By what name does Sibyl Vane know Dorian Gray?
- A. Prince Charming
- B. Prince Phillip
- C. Romeo
- D. Don Juan

C 2. What does Jim demand to know from his mother before he leaves for Australia?
- A. He wants to know if she ever cared about him at all.
- B. He demands to know why she seems to have such hatred toward him.
- C. He demands to know whether or not she was ever married to his father.
- D. He demands to know the name of the man who is courting his sister.

A 3. What does it mean to be "good," according to Lord Henry?
- A. To be good is to be in harmony with oneself.
- B. To be good is to be kind and charitable to others.
- C. To be good is to do one's best to maintain youth and beauty at all costs.
- D. To be good means to work hard for what you have.

C 4. When Lord Henry and Basil accompany Dorian to the theatre, what happens to make Dorian angry?
- A. They are late arriving from dinner and are not allowed to enter during the show.
- B. That night's performance has been cancelled.
- C. Sibyl's performance is terrible. Lord Henry and Basil leave during the show.
- D. Sibyl is so convincing as Juliet that Dorian has become jealous of "Romeo."

B 5. What explanation does Sibyl Vane offer Dorian regarding her performance?
- A. She believes that she has given the best performance of her life now that she knows what it is to truly love.
- B. She no longer desires to live the lives of her characters, and she wishes to live in the real world with Dorian. She now sees the actors on the stage and not the characters she used to see. This reality has spoiled her acting.
- C. She fell ill suddenly and was not able to perform.
- D. She was only doing as she had always done; Dorian's jealousy is outrageous.

D 6. What is Dorian's reaction to Sibyl's explanation for her poor performance?
- A. He slaps her and throws her to the floor.
- B. He apologizes for his insane jealousy and vows to trust her from then on.
- C. He pulls her close and tells her nothing could ever come between them.
- D. He says that he is no longer in love with her, and he will never see her again.

B 7. What does Dorian realize when he sees the changes in the painting?
- A. He realizes he made the right choice not to marry Sybil.
- B. Dorian realizes how cruel he has been to Sibyl Vane, and he vows that he will make it up to her.
- C. He realizes he must destroy the painting before it destroys him.
- D. Basil must have tampered with the painting because he is angry with Dorian.

A 8. What news is in Lord Henry's letter that Dorian does not open?
- A. Lord Henry's note says he has learned that Sibyl Vane died in an incident at the theater.
- B. Lord Henry's wife has asked for a divorce and is leaving him.
- C. Basil Hallward is missing.
- D. The Duchess is so angry with Dorian for standing her up that she vowed to ruin his reputation.

A 9. What choice does Dorian Gray make after Lord Henry points out how fortunate Dorian is that someone loved him so much as to kill herself for him?
- A. Dorian chooses to follow his passions and to allow the painting to bear the burden of his shame.
- B. Dorian chooses to see the Duchess immediately to get Sibyl out of his mind.
- C. Dorian vows to create a large memorial to Sibyl Vane.
- D. Dorian vows to never be cruel to anyone again.

C 10. What does Dorian believe would be a real pleasure to watch?
- A. He believes that it would be a real pleasure to watch Lord Henry beg his wife not to leave him.
- B. He believes that it would be a real pleasure to see the Duchess weeping and asking for forgiveness.
- C. He believes that it would be a real pleasure to watch the painting change while he physically remains the same.
- D. He believes that it would be a real pleasure to see future actresses benefiting from the Sibyl Vane memorial fund.

ORAL READING EVALUATION- *The Picture of Dorian Gray*

Name _____ Class____ Date _____

SKILL	EXCELLENT	GOOD	AVERAGE	FAIR	POOR
Fluency	5	4	3	2	1
Clarity	5	4	3	2	1
Audibility	5	4	3	2	1
Pronunciation	5	4	3	2	1
_____	5	4	3	2	1
_____	5	4	3	2	1

Total _____ Grade _____

Comments:

LESSON SIX

Objectives
1. To review the main events and ideas for Chapters 9-10
2. To practice public speaking skills
3. To connect current events (scandals) to the novel
4. To preview the study questions and vocabulary for Chapters 11-12
5. To read Chapters 11-12

Activity 1
Discuss the answers to the study questions for Chapters 9-10 as previously directed.

Activity 2
Ask each student to give a brief oral report about the non-fiction article(s) he/she read. Your criteria for evaluating this report will vary depending on the level of your students and the instructions you gave for this assignment.

After all reports are given, take a few minutes to hold a short class discussion about all the information presented, focusing on comparisons, contrasts, comments, etc.

Activity 3
Write the word "dandyism" on the board and ask students if they can give any kind of a definition of the term.

A **dandy** is a man who places particular importance on physical appearance, refined language, and the cultivation of leisurely hobbies.

How does this term (attributing it to both male and female "dandies") apply to the non-fiction articles that the students just presented to the class? Why might "dandies" be both admired and despised by the middle class? Apply this term and these questions to Dorian Gray.

How does the character of Dorian Gray reflect the subject matter of the non-fiction articles that students have presented?

Activity 4
Tell students to do the pre-reading work and reading for Chapters 11-12 prior to the next class. If time remains in this class period, students may begin working on this assignment.

LESSON SEVEN

Objectives
1. To review the main events, ideas, and vocabulary for Chapters 11-12
2. To demonstrate and evaluate reading comprehension through taking a quiz
3. To research in preparation for Writing Assignment #1
4. To practice writing to inform
5. To preview the study questions and vocabulary for Chapters 13-14
6. To read Chapters 13-14

Activity 1
Discuss the answers to the study questions from Chapters 11-12 as previously directed.

Activity 2
Discuss or post the answers to the vocabulary worksheet for Chapters 11-12 so students have the correct answers for study purposes.

Activity 3
Distribute the quizzes for Chapters 9-12 and give students ample time to complete them. Collect the quizzes for grading or grade them orally in class.

Activity 4
Distribute Writing Assignment #1. Discuss the directions in detail. Take students to the library/media center to do research for this assignment.

Topic: People of leisure had plenty of time to devote to the study of many areas of interest. Below is a list of topics Dorian Gray studied. Have students choose one of these topics to explore on their own. Students should refer to the specifics of Chapter Eleven for their research.

Embroidered clothing
Tapestries
Jewels and gemstones
Perfumes
The rituals of Roman Catholicism
Mysticism
Music

Activity 5
Tell students to do the pre-reading work and reading for Chapters 13-14 prior to the next class meeting.

The Picture of Dorian Gray QUIZ CHAPTERS 9-12

I. Multiple Choice

1. Who does Basil blame for the changes in Dorian?
    A. Sibyl Vane
    B. Lord Henry
    C. Himself
    D. The Duchess

2. Dorian threatens never to speak to Basil again. Why?
    A. Dorian doesn't want Basil to see the painting, so he threatens never to speak to Basil again if Basil looks at it.
    B. Basil blames Dorian for Sibyl's death and wants Dorian to repent his sins.
    C. Basil wants to tell Lord Henry to stay away from Dorian.
    D. Basil threatens to tell Dorian's grandfather about the difficulties Dorian is going through.

3. What does Basil want to do with the portrait of Dorian he painted?
    A. Basil wants to exhibit the portrait in Paris.
    B. An art collector in Paris wants to buy the portrait; he wants Dorian to sell it.
    C. He wants to buy it back from Dorian to keep for himself.
    D. He wants to destroy it because it shows too much of his own soul.

4. Where does Dorian Gray decide to hide the painting?
    A. He hides it under his bed.
    B. He hides it in the basement.
    C. He hides it in a secret room behind the drawing room wainscoting.
    D. He hides the painting in an old schoolroom at the top of his house.

5. What does the coroner give as the official cause of Sibyl Vane's death?
    A. It was officially proclaimed a suicide.
    B. It was officially proclaimed death by natural causes.
    C. It was officially proclaimed an accidental death.
    D. It was officially proclaimed a murder.

6. What becomes a huge influence over Dorian Gray's life?
   A. Dorian has a secret relationship with the Duchess for several years.
   B. Dorian is fascinated with the way the painting changed; he just sits and watches it.
   C. The book that Lord Henry gave Dorian has a huge influence over Dorian's behavior.
   D. Dorian has a torrid affair with Lord Henry's wife.

7. Why do people tend to disbelieve the rumors about Dorian Gray?
   A. His donations to charity are very generous.
   B. He piously attends Mass daily.
   C. His youthful beauty keeps people from believing the worst about him.
   D. He is a very dedicated worker who never neglects his duties.

8. Which is NOT one of the activities or interests that managed to capture Dorian Gray's attention in his study of the senses?
   A. Zoology
   B. Catholic ritual
   C. Gemstones
   D. Tapestries

9. What is it that Basil wishes to speak to Dorian about before leaving?
   A. He wants to express his admiration for Dorian.
   B. He wants Dorian to accompany him on his trip.
   C. He wants to know the truth about the terrible rumors surrounding Dorian's moral character.
   D. He wants to warn him once again to stay away from Lord Henry's influence.

10. What does Basil claim that he would have to see before he could believe anything he's heard about Dorian's activities?
    A. Basil claims that he would have to see Dorian's soul.
    B. Basil claims he would have to read Dorian's diary.
    C. Basil claims he would have to see the portrain he painted of Dorian.
    D. Basil claims he would have to speak to Dorian's servants.

The Picture of Dorian Gray QUIZ CHAPTERS 9-12 Answer Key

I. Multiple Choice

B 1. Who does Basil blame for the changes in Dorian?
- A. Sibyl Vane
- B. Lord Henry
- C. Himself
- D. The Duchess

A 2. Dorian threatens never to speak to Basil again. Why?
- A. Dorian doesn't want Basil to see the painting, so he threatens never to speak to Basil again if Basil looks at it.
- B. Basil blames Dorian for Sibyl's death and wants Dorian to repent his sins.
- C. Basil wants to tell Lord Henry to stay away from Dorian.
- D. Basil threatens to tell Dorian's grandfather about the difficulties Dorian is going through.

A 3. What does Basil want to do with the portrait of Dorian he painted?
- A. Basil wants to exhibit the portrait in Paris.
- B. An art collector in Paris wants to buy the portrait; he wants Dorian to sell it.
- C. He wants to buy it back from Dorian to keep for himself.
- D. He wants to destroy it because it shows too much of his own soul.

D 4. Where does Dorian Gray decide to hide the painting?
- A. He hides it under his bed.
- B. He hides it in the basement.
- C. He hides it in a secret room behind the drawing room wainscoting.
- D. He hides the painting in an old schoolroom at the top of his house.

C 5. What does the coroner give as the official cause of Sibyl Vane's death?
- A. It was officially proclaimed a suicide.
- B. It was officially proclaimed death by natural causes.
- C. It was officially proclaimed an accidental death.
- D. It was officially proclaimed a murder.

C 6.   What becomes a huge influence over Dorian Gray's life?
   A. Dorian has a secret relationship with the Duchess for several years.
   B. Dorian is fascinated with the way the painting changed; he just sits and watches it.
   C. The book that Lord Henry gave Dorian has a huge influence over Dorian's behavior.
   D. Dorian has a torrid affair with Lord Henry's wife.

C 7.   Why do people tend to disbelieve the rumors about Dorian Gray?
   A. His donations to charity are very generous.
   B. He piously attends Mass daily.
   C. His youthful beauty keeps people from believing the worst about him.
   D. He is a very dedicated worker who never neglects his duties.

A 8.   Which is NOT one of the activities or interests that managed to capture Dorian Gray's attention in his study of the senses?
   A. Zoology
   B. Catholic ritual
   C. Gemstones
   D. Tapestries

C 9.   What is it that Basil wishes to speak to Dorian about before leaving?
   A. He wants to express his admiration for Dorian.
   B. He wants Dorian to accompany him on his trip.
   C. He wants to know the truth about the terrible rumors surrounding Dorian's moral character.
   D. He wants to warn him once again to stay away from Lord Henry's influence.

A 10.   What does Basil claim that he would have to see before he could believe anything he's heard about Dorian's activities?
   A. Basil claims that he would have to see Dorian's soul.
   B. Basil claims he would have to read Dorian's diary.
   C. Basil claims he would have to see the portrain he painted of Dorian.
   D. Basil claims he would have to speak to Dorian's servants.

WRITING ASSIGNMENT #1 *The Picture of Dorian Gray*

PROMPT
In the novel *The Picture of Dorian Gray*, Dorian had plenty of time to explore his interests. For this assignment you will research one of Dorian's many interests and write an essay providing information on your chosen topic and telling why Dorian found it interesting.

PREWRITING
Select one of the following topics:

  Embroidered clothing
  Tapestries
  Jewels and gemstones
  Rituals of Roman Catholicism
  Mysticism
  Music

Refer to Chapter 11 in *The Picture of Dorian Gray*, and review any information regarding your topic. Gather information from the library, Internet, or through interviewing someone who is an expert on your topic.

DRAFTING
Write an essay in which you describe one of the avenues of interest that Dorian Gray explored. Using supportive evidence from Wilde's text and information gleaned from your research, give two reasons why Dorian might have found this topic interesting. What seemed to be so fascinating about it? Are you as fascinated with this area of study as Dorian might have been? Finally, make connections to modern examples of the subject (contemporary jewelry, New Age mysticism, hip-hop music, designer clothes or perfumes, etc.) and demonstrate how people today are just as fascinated as ever.

PROMPT
When you finish the rough draft of your paper, ask a student whose opinions you trust to read it. After reading your rough draft, he/she should tell you what he/she liked best about your work, which parts were difficult to understand, and ways in which your work could be improved. Reread your paper considering your critic's comments and make the corrections you think are necessary.

PROOFREADING
Do a final proofreading of your paper, double-checking your grammar, spelling, organization, and the clarity of your ideas.

WRITING EVALUATION FORM - *The Picture of Dorian Gray*

Name _____ Date _____

Grade _____

Circle One For Each Item:

Grammar: correct errors noted on paper

Spelling: correct errors noted on paper

Punctuation: correct errors noted on paper

Legibility: excellent   good   fair   poor

_____   excellent   good   fair   poor

_____   excellent   good   fair   poor

Strengths:

Weaknesses:

Comments/Suggestions:

LESSON EIGHT

Objectives
1. To review the main events, ideas, and vocabulary for Chapters 13-14
2. To demonstrate a working knowledge of the *doppelganger*
3. To acquaint students with Swiss psychiatrist Carl Jung and the *collective unconscious*, in particular the *shadow*
4. To practice cooperative learning skills through group work
5. To practice public speaking through oral presentations
6. To preview the study questions and vocabulary for Chapters 15-16
7. To read Chapters 15-16

Activity 1
Discuss the answers to the study questions for Chapters 13-14 as previously directed.

Activity 2
Discuss or post the answers to the vocabulary worksheet for Chapters 13-14 so students have the correct answers for study purposes.

Activity 3
Although Swiss psychiatrist Carl Jung did not coin the terms "collective unconscious" and "archetypes" until 1919 in his essay "Instinct and the Unconscious," Oscar Wilde's *The Picture of Dorian Gray* (1891) can be used to study Jung's concept of what he called the "shadow," or hidden portion of a person's personality or soul. While Jung's "shadow" does have many positive qualities that are merely hidden from consciousness, literature if filled with "doppelgangers" or "dark twins" that could be analyzed as the dark side of the shadow.

Review the concept of the "doppelganger" from Lesson One and relate Jung's ideas about the "shadow" to Robert Louis Stevenson's "Markheim." Other doppelganger stories that could be explored to are *Dr. Jekyll and Mr. Hyde* by Robert Louis Stevenson, "William Wilson" by Edgar Allan Poe, *Lord of the Flies* by William Golding, or "Charles" by Shirley Jackson.

Ask student for ideas from modern movies that portray this theme (*The Mask* starring Jim Carey, *Batman*--especially the 2005 *Batman Begins*, and *Spider-Man* are good examples. Actually, any super-hero movie in which the villain hides behind a mask is a representation of the shadow.) A wonderful scene depicting man's struggle with the shadow is in the first of the *Spider-Man* movies starring Tobey Maguire and Willem Dafoe. Harry Osborn (Willem Dafoe) has been "split" into two distinct personalities, one of them being the evil Green Goblin, and there is a scene in which the Green Goblin (depicted in a mirror) goads Harry Osborn to destroy the men who took his company. If possible, playing a clip from the film might give students a clearer understanding of the "doppelganger."

Activity 4
In Chapter 12, Basil Hallward, after hearing vicious rumors about Dorian Gray, wonders if he ever really knew Dorian at all--and remarks that for him to truly know Dorian, he would have to see the young man's soul. In response to Basil's statement, Dorian sneers and says, "You shall see it yourself, to-night! . . . You have chattered enough about corruption. Now you shall look on it face to face."

On the next page are seven quotations from Carl Jung's work relating to Jung's concept of the "shadow." Divide the class into groups, one for each quotation. You may use all seven quotations or select those you wish to use.

Students should first discuss what Jung is saying about the hidden portion of the psyche in their particular passages, then relate the main idea(s) to Oscar Wilde's novel. Each group should come up with a specific event or scene in the novel that fits the main idea of Jung's words. Groups should be able to explain why the selected scene is an appropriate representation of Jung's ideas, and then illustrate the scene, using a quotation from the Jung passage as a caption.

After completing the pictures and discussions, each group will share its passage and its findings with the rest of the class.

Activity 5
Tell students to do the pre-reading work and reading for Chapters 15-16 prior to the next class.

PASSAGES FROM THE WORKS OF CARL JUNG *The Picture of Dorian Gray*

Unfortunately there can be no doubt that man is, on the whole, less good than he imagines himself or wants to be. Everyone carries a shadow, and the less it is embodied in the individual's conscious life, the blacker and denser it is. If an inferiority is conscious, one always has a chance to correct it. Furthermore, it is constantly in contact with other interests, so that it is continually subjected to modifications. But if it is repressed and isolated from consciousness, it never gets corrected.
  "*Psychology and Religion*" *(1938). In CW 11: Psychology and Religion: West and East. P. 131.*

We carry our past with us, to wit, the primitive and inferior man with his desires and emotions, and it is only with an enormous effort that we can detach ourselves from this burden. If it comes to a neurosis, we invariably have to deal with a considerably intensified shadow. And if such a person wants to be cured, it is necessary to find a way in which his conscious personality and his shadow can live together.
  "*Answer to Job*" *(1952). In CW 11: Psychology and Religion: West and East. P.12.*

To remain a child too long is childish, but it is just as childish to move away and then assume that childhood no longer exists because we do not see it. But if we return to the "children's land" we succumb to the fear of becoming childish, because we do not understand that everything of psychic origin has a double face. One face looks forward, the other back. It is ambivalent and therefore symbolic, like all living reality.
  "*Psychology and Alchemy*" *(1944). CW 12. P. 74.*

Just as we tend to assume that the world is as we see it, we naively suppose that people are as we imagine them to be. In this latter case, unfortunately, there is no scientific test that would prove the discrepancy between perception and reality. Although the possibility of gross deception is infinitely greater here than in our perception of the physical world, we still go on naively projecting our own psychology into our fellow human beings. In this way everyone creates for himself a series of more or less imaginary relationships based essentially on projection.
  "*General Aspects of Dream Psychology*" *(1916). In CW 8: The Structure and Dynamics of the Psyche. P. 507.*

The change of character brought about by the uprush of collective forces is amazing. A gentle and reasonable being can be transformed into a maniac or a savage beast. One is always inclined to lay the blame on external circumstances, but nothing could explode in us if it had not been there. As a matter of fact, we are constantly living on the edge of a volcano, and there is, so far as we know, no way of protecting ourselves from a possible outburst that will destroy everybody within reach. It is certainly a good thing to preach reason and common sense, but what if you have a lunatic asylum for an audience or a crowd in a collective frenzy? There is not much difference between them because the madman and the mob are both moved by impersonal, overwhelming forces.
  "*Psychology and Religion*" *(1938). In CW 11: Psychology and Religion: West and East. P. 25.*

To confront a person with his shadow is to show him his own light. Once one has experienced a few times what it is like to stand judgingly between the opposites, one begins to understand what is meant by the self. Anyone who perceives his shadow and his light simultaneously sees himself from two sides and thus gets in the middle.
  "*Good and Evil in Analytical Psychology*" *(1959). In CW 10: Civilization in Transition. P. 872.*

Good does not become better by being exaggerated, but worse, and a small evil becomes a big one through being disregarded and repressed. The shadow is very much a part of human nature, and it is only at night that no shadows exist.
"A Psychological Approach to the Dogma of the Trinity" (1942). In CW 11:
  Psychology and Religion: West and East. P. 286.

LESSON NINE

Objectives
1. To review the main events, ideas, and vocabulary for Chapters 15-16
2. To demonstrate reading comprehension through taking a quiz
3. To practice and evaluate public speaking skills
4. To preview the study questions and vocabulary for Chapters 17-18
5. To read Chapters 17-18

Activity 1
Discuss the answers to the study questions for Chapters 15-16 as previously directed.

Review the study questions for Chapters 17-18 while students have their study guides out.

Activity 2
Discuss or post the answers to the vocabulary worksheet for Chapters 15-16 so students have the correct answers for study purposes.

Complete the vocabulary worksheet for Chapters 17-18 orally together in class.

Activity 3
Distribute the quizzes for Chapters 13-16, and give students ample time to complete them. Collect the quizzes for grading or check them orally.

Activity 4
Read Chapters 17-18 orally in class. If you have not completed the oral reading evaluations, do so today since this will be the last opportunity to do so in this unit.

If you do not finish this reading assignment in class, students should do so for homework prior to the next class meeting.

The Picture of Dorian Gray QUIZ CHAPTERS 13-16

I. Multiple Choice

1. What does Basil see when he looks at the portrait he painted of Dorian Gray?
    A. Basil sees a bloody knife in Dorian's hand.
    B. Basil sees an aging man who has the look of a satyr.
    C. Basil sees an aging man with the look of contempt in his eyes.
    D. Basil sees no changes; only Dorian can see the changes in the painting.

2. What does Dorian Gray do to Basil?
    A. Dorian breaks down in tears and prays for Basil's forgiveness.
    B. Dorian viciously stabs Basil in the neck with an artist's knife.
    C. Dorian tells Basil to leave and never return.
    D. Dorian shoves Basil out of the room, and Basil accidentally falls down the stairs and breaks his neck.

3. What does Dorian do to provide himself with an alibi regarding Basil's death?
    A. Dorian goes to the local brothel and pays one of the women to say he had been with her all night.
    B. Dorian goes outside and bangs on his door to awaken his servants. In doing so his servants will provide him with an alibi that he returned home after Basil had gone.
    C. Dorian goes to Lord Henry and asks him to provide Dorian with an alibi.
    D. Dorian goes to the club and pretends to be upset because Basil has not joined him as planned.

4. As Dorian sketches, what seems to appear in all of his drawings?
    A. Basil Hallward's face begins to appear in all of his drawings.
    B. The face of the portrait begins to appear in all of his drawings.
    C. Sibyl Vane's face begins to appear in all of his drawings.
    D. His own youthful face begins to appear in all of his drawings.

5. What request does Dorian Gray make of Alan Campbell?
    A. Dorian wants Alan to claim responsibility for Basil's death.
    B. Dorian wants Alan to accompany him to Paris and pretend to be Basil Hallward.
    C. Dorian wants Alan to pose as Basil for several days around London so that people will think that Basil is still alive; meanwhile, Dorian will go to Paris, creating an alibi.
    D. Dorian asks Alan Campbell to dispose of Basil's body.

6. What is Dorian's mood when he attends Lady Narborough's party?
   A. He is nervous and jittery; Lord Henry remarks on his behavior.
   B. He becomes loud and obnoxious after drinking far too much.
   C. He is cantankerous and argues loudly with everyone.
   D. He is surprisingly calm despite what had happened with Basil.

7. Whom does Lady Narbourough accuse of being "extremely wicked"?
   A. Lord Henry
   B. Her husband
   C. Basil Hallward
   D. Dorian Gray

8. What does Lord Henry ask Dorian at Lady Narbourough's party that makes Dorian nervous?
   A. Lord Henry asks if Dorian has seen Basil; no one has seen him in the last 24 hours.
   B. Lord Henry asks if he could see the painting of Dorian just once more.
   C. Lord Henry asks Dorian where he went after leaving early the night before.
   D. Lord Henry asks if Basil is coming to the party.

9. Who is the drunken sailor who accused Dorian Gray in the street?
   A. The drunken sailor is James Vane, Sibyl Vane's older brother.
   B. The drunken sailor is Basil's son.
   C. The drunken sailor is a former friend of Dorian whose reputation was ruined.
   D. The drunken sailor is Lord Henry's cousin.

10. Why doesn't the drunken sailor shoot Dorian Gray?
    A. Dorian looks to young to be the man who caused Sibyl Vane to commit suicide.
    B. Lord Henry takes the gun away from the sailor before he has a change to shoot Dorian.
    C. Dorian looks to old to be the man who caused Sibyl Vane to commit suicide.
    D. Dorian disarms the sailor and takes him to the police.

The Picture of Dorian Gray QUIZ CHAPTERS 13-16 Answer Key

I. Multiple Choice

B 1. What does Basil see when he looks at the portrait he painted of Dorian Gray?
- A. Basil sees a bloody knife in Dorian's hand.
- B. Basil sees an aging man who has the look of a satyr.
- C. Basil sees an aging man with the look of contempt in his eyes.
- D. Basil sees no changes; only Dorian can see the changes in the painting.

B 2. What does Dorian Gray do to Basil?
- A. Dorian breaks down in tears and prays for Basil's forgiveness.
- B. Dorian viciously stabs Basil in the neck with an artist's knife.
- C. Dorian tells Basil to leave and never return.
- D. Dorian shoves Basil out of the room, and Basil accidentally falls down the stairs and breaks his neck.

B 3. What does Dorian do to provide himself with an alibi regarding Basil's death?
- A. Dorian goes to the local brothel and pays one of the women to say he had been with her all night.
- B. Dorian goes outside and bangs on his door to awaken his servants. In doing so his servants will provide him with an alibi that he returned home after Basil had gone.
- C. Dorian goes to Lord Henry and asks him to provide Dorian with an alibi.
- D. Dorian goes to the club and pretends to be upset because Basil has not joined him as planned.

A 4. As Dorian sketches, what seems to appear in all of his drawings?
- A. Basil Hallward's face begins to appear in all of his drawings.
- B. The face of the portrait begins to appear in all of his drawings.
- C. Sibyl Vane's face begins to appear in all of his drawings.
- D. His own youthful face begins to appear in all of his drawings.

D 5. What request does Dorian Gray make of Alan Campbell?
- A. Dorian wants Alan to claim responsibility for Basil's death.
- B. Dorian wants Alan to accompany him to Paris and pretend to be Basil Hallward.
- C. Dorian wants Alan to pose as Basil for several days around London so that people will think that Basil is still alive; meanwhile, Dorian will go to Paris, creating an alibi.
- D. Dorian asks Alan Campbell to dispose of Basil's body.

D 6.   What is Dorian's mood when he attends Lady Narborough's party?
   A. He is nervous and jittery; Lord Henry remarks on his behavior.
   B. He becomes loud and obnoxious after drinking far too much.
   C. He is cantankerous and argues loudly with everyone.
   D. He is surprisingly calm despite what had happened with Basil.

A 7.   Whom does Lady Narbourough accuse of being "extremely wicked"?
   A. Lord Henry
   B. Her husband
   C. Basil Hallward
   D. Dorian Gray

C 8.   What does Lord Henry ask Dorian at Lady Narbourough's party that makes Dorian nervous?
   A. Lord Henry asks if Dorian has seen Basil; no one has seen him in the last 24 hours.
   B. Lord Henry asks if he could see the painting of Dorian just once more.
   C. Lord Henry asks Dorian where he went after leaving early the night before.
   D. Lord Henry asks if Basil is coming to the party.

A 9.   Who is the drunken sailor who accused Dorian Gray in the street?
   A. The drunken sailor is James Vane, Sibyl Vane's older brother.
   B. The drunken sailor is Basil's son.
   C. The drunken sailor is a former friend of Dorian whose reputation was ruined.
   D. The drunken sailor is Lord Henry's cousin.

A 10.   Why doesn't the drunken sailor shoot Dorian Gray?
   A. Dorian looks to young to be the man who caused Sibyl Vane to commit suicide.
   B. Lord Henry takes the gun away from the sailor before he has a change to shoot Dorian.
   C. Dorian looks to old to be the man who caused Sibyl Vane to commit suicide.
   D. Dorian disarms the sailor and takes him to the police.

LESSON TEN

Objectives
1. To review the main events and ideas for Chapters 17-18
2. To brainstorm ideas in preparation for Writing Assignment #2
3. To demonstrate cooperative learning skills through planning in groups
4. To preview the study questions and vocabulary for Chapters 19-20
5. To read Chapters 19-20

Activity 1
Discuss the answers to the study questions for Chapters 17-18 as previously directed.

Activity 2
Distribute Writing Assignment #2 and discuss the directions in detail. Today is a *brainstorming session only*, and students will be working in groups of 4 or 5. Their task is to create a scandal sheet (a la *The National Enquirer*) using the various characters that Basil Hallward referred to in his accusation of Dorin Gray in Chapter 12 of *The Picture of Dorian Gray*. According to Basil, what happened to each of the characters? Each student is to choose one of Dorian's unfortunate acquaintances and create TWO articles for the group's "newspaper" about this person: one article depicting a social occasion which involves Dorian Gray and a second article depicting this person's fall from social grace. Give students ample time to think about their characters and brainstorm ideas. Students will actually work on the *writing* of this assignment in Lesson Twelve.

Activity 3
When groups have a clear idea of what they want to do for their scandal sheet, students may work individually and independently on polishing their Writing Assignment #1, which will be due in the next class meeting.

Activity 4
Tell students to do the pre-reading work and reading for Chapters 19-20 prior to your next class meeting. If time remains in this class period, students may begin this assignment.

WRITING ASSIGNMENT #2 *The Picture of Dorian Gray*

PROMPT

In Chapter 12 of *The Picture of Dorian Gray*, Basil Hallward presents the rumors he has heard about Dorian Gray's activities and the negative effects he has had on his former acquaintances. Referring to Basil's accusations, your group will create a scandal sheet (a la *The National Enquirer*) complete with articles about these characters. Each member of the group will choose a character and write two articles: one about this person's association with Dorian Gray in society, and another about this person's fall from social grace. You will be putting these articles together in a group "newspaper" or scandal sheet.

PREWRITING

All of the following used to be close friends of Dorian Gray; however, all have had their reputations and/or their lives destroyed through their association with Dorian. The following list contains sinister insinuations regarding the characters' interactions with Dorian Gray. It is up to you to create the story for the readers of your newspaper. With your group members, decide which character each group member will be assigned. Each group member should have a different character, with no duplications.

Duke of Berwick: leaves the room at the club as soon as Dorian walks in; Dorian knows all about his life

Lord Stavely: used to be friends with Dorian and said Dorian had artistic tastes, but no pure-minded girl or chaste woman should ever be alone with him

Young boy in the Guards: committed suicide

Sir Henry Ashton: was forced to leave England with a tarnished name

Adrian Singleton: forged his friend's name on a bill and became an opium addict

Duke of Perth: has a ruined reputation among society

Lord Kent's only son: married a prostitute and the family is ashamed of him

Sibyl Vane: committed suicide after Dorian Gray broke their engagement

Alan Campbell: allowed himself to be blackmailed by Dorian rather than have some sordid secret exposed; he later committed suicide

Lady Gwendolen: after a terrible scandal, her children were taken away from her and no one would be seen in public with her

Lady Gloucester: made an infamous death-bed confession that involved Dorian's name

Basil Hallward: no one (except the reader) knows what happened to him; he used to be a friend of Dorian Gray but has disappeared

DRAFTING

Write two newspaper articles about your chosen character. The first article should be a "who's who in society" type that depicts a particular social function that the person attended. The second is to be a scandalous story about his/her fall from social grace. For each, be sure to use active verbs and a strong lead to grab your reader's attention.

PROMPT
When you finish the rough draft of your articles, ask a student whose opinion you trust to read it. After reading your rough draft, he/she should tell you what he/she liked best about your work, which parts were difficult to understand, and ways in which your work could be improved. Reread your articles considering your critic's comments and make the corrections you think are necessary.

PROOFREADING
Do a final proofreading of your articles double-checking your grammar, spelling, organization, and the clarity of your ideas.

LESSON ELEVEN

<u>Objectives</u>
1. To review the main events, ideas, and vocabulary from Chapters 19-20
2. To demonstrate reading comprehension by taking a quiz
3. To analyze the poem "False Friend"
4. To make connections between the main ideas of the poem and the novel

<u>Activity 1</u>
Discuss the answers to the study questions for Chapters 19-20 as previously directed.

<u>Activity 2</u>
Discuss or post the answers to the vocabulary worksheet for Chapters 19-20 so students have the correct answers for study purposes.

<u>Activity 3</u>
Distribute the quizzes for Chapters 17-20. Give students ample time to complete the quizzes, then collect them for grading or grade them orally in class.

<u>Activity 4</u>
Distribute copies of the poem "False Friend" by Susan Woodward and the corresponding questions. Read the poem aloud first, and then have students reread it silently to themselves. While reading, students should RHA (Read, Highlight, and Annotate) the poem.

READ for understanding; briefly summarize each stanza

HIGHLIGHT poetic devices found in the work (one color) and lines that can link to *The Picture of Dorian Gray* (another color)

ANNOTATE (take notes in the margin) to identify the poetic device and briefly explain how its use enhances the meaning of the poem AND make connections between the poem and Wilde's novel *The Picture of Dorian Gray*

Have students answer the questions as well as create an illustration for the poem that best explores its overall meaning.

After students RHA the poem, discuss their notes, responses to the questions, and illustrations as a class.

<u>NOTE:</u>
If you have access to a digital camera, ask students to bring in props or costumes that could be used for paparazzi photos to be taken in the next class.

The Picture of Dorian Gray QUIZ CHAPTERS 17-20

I. Multiple Choice

1. When Gladys tells Lord Henry he values beauty far too much, what is his response?
    A. He thinks it is better to be beautiful than to be good--but acknowledges it is better to be good than ugly.
    B. He thinks it is better to be wealthy than to be good--but acknowledges it is better to be beautiful than ugly.
    C. He admits it is better to be ugly than to be evil--but acknowledges it is better to be good than ugly.
    D. He thinks it is better to be good than to be beautiful--but acknowledges it is better to be beautiful than ugly.

2. What did Dorian Gray believe he had seen through the window of the conservatory?
    A. He had seen the face of Alan Campbell watching him.
    B. He had seen the face of James Vane watching him.
    C. He had seen the face of Basil Hallward watching him.
    D. He had seen the face of Sibyl Vane watching him.

3. What does Dorian Gray blame for raising "such fearful phantoms" that keep him in his house for three days?
    A. He blames his conscience.
    B. He blames James Vane.
    C. He blames Basil Hallward.
    D. He blames Lord Henry's influence.

4. What happens that Dorian Gray proclaims to be a "bad omen"?
    A. Dorian accidentally shoots a man hiding in the thicket.
    B. Sir Geoffrey is struck by lightning while hunting.
    C. Lord Henry disappears during the hunting trip.
    D. Sir Geoffrey accidently shoots a man hiding in the thicket.

5. Who is the man in the thicket?
    A. Sir Geoffrey
    B. Lord Henry
    C. Alan Campbell
    D. James Vane

6. Who is Hetty?
    A. Hetty is an actress who worked with Sibyl Vane, and she knows Dorian's secret.
    B. Hetty is Dorian's servant with whom Dorian plans to run away.
    C. Hetty is a young peasant girl with whom Dorian plans to run away.
    D. Hetty is Lord Henry's niece with whom Dorian plans to run away.

7. What becomes of Alan Campbell?
    A. Alan Campbell commits suicide.
    B. Alan Campbell is arrested for his part in Basil's death.
    C. Alan Campbell becomes an opium addict.
    D. Alan Campbell leaves England to go to Australia.

8. What does Dorian tell Lord Henry that Henry immediately dismisses as impossible to believe?
    A. Dorian tells Lord Henry that he killed Basil.
    B. Dorian tells Lord Henry that he is leaving England forever.
    C. Dorian tells Lord Henry that he truly loves Hetty.
    D. Dorian tells Lord Henry that he is in love with Lord Henry's wife.

9. What happens to Dorian Gray?
    A. Dorian is killed by Lord Henry when Henry sees the painting.
    B. Dorian accidentally falls on the knife that he used to kill Basil.
    C. Dorian is arrested for the murder of Basil Hallward and is hanged.
    D. Dorian dies while trying to destroy the portrait.

10. Why does Dorian go to his portrait while thingking of Hetty Merton?
    A. Dorian goes to pack the painting away so he can start over without the painting reminding him of his old ways.
    B. Dorain goes to destroy the painting.
    C. Dorian believes because he is trying to change the portrait will also change.
    D. Dorian goes to move the painting to another room in the house so he will never have to see it again.

The Picture of Dorian Gray QUIZ CHAPTERS 17-20 Answer Key

I. Multiple Choice

A 1. When Gladys tells Lord Henry he values beauty far too much, what is his response?
   A. He thinks it is better to be beautiful than to be good--but acknowledges it is better to be good than ugly.
   B. He thinks it is better to be wealthy than to be good--but acknowledges it is better to be beautiful than ugly.
   C. He admits it is better to be ugly than to be evil--but acknowledges it is better to be good than ugly.
   D. He thinks it is better to be good than to be beautiful--but acknowledges it is better to be beautiful than ugly.

B 2. What did Dorian Gray believe he had seen through the window of the conservatory?
   A. He had seen the face of Alan Campbell watching him.
   B. He had seen the face of James Vane watching him.
   C. He had seen the face of Basil Hallward watching him.
   D. He had seen the face of Sibyl Vane watching him.

A 3. What does Dorian Gray blame for raising "such fearful phantoms" that keep him in his house for three days?
   A. He blames his conscience.
   B. He blames James Vane.
   C. He blames Basil Hallward.
   D. He blames Lord Henry's influence.

D 4. What happens that Dorian Gray proclaims to be a "bad omen"?
   A. Dorian accidently shoots a man hiding in the thicket.
   B. Sir Geoffrey is struck by lightning while hunting.
   C. Lord Henry disappears during the hunting trip.
   D. Sir Geoffrey accidentally shoots a man hiding in the thicket.

D 5. Who is the man in the thicket?
   A. Sir Geoffrey
   B. Lord Henry
   C. Alan Campbell
   D. James Vane

C 6. Who is Hetty?
- A. Hetty is an actress who worked with Sibyl Vane, and she knows Dorian's secret.
- B. Hetty is Dorian's servant with whom Dorian plans to run away.
- C. Hetty is a young peasant girl with whom Dorian plans to run away.
- D. Hetty is Lord Henry's niece with whom Dorian plans to run away.

A 7. What becomes of Alan Campbell?
- A. Alan Campbell commits suicide.
- B. Alan Campbell is arrested for his part in Basil's death.
- C. Alan Campbell becomes an opium addict.
- D. Alan Campbell leaves England to go to Australia.

A 8. What does Dorian tell Lord Henry that Henry immediately dismisses as impossible to believe?
- A. Dorian tells Lord Henry that he killed Basil.
- B. Dorian tells Lord Henry that he is leaving England forever.
- C. Dorian tells Lord Henry that he truly loves Hetty.
- D. Dorian tells Lord Henry that he is in love with Lord Henry's wife.

D 9. What happens to Dorian Gray?
- A. Dorian is killed by Lord Henry when Henry sees the painting.
- B. Dorian accidentally falls on the knife that he used to kill Basil.
- C. Dorian is arrested for the murder of Basil Hallward and is hanged.
- D. Dorian dies while trying to destroy the portrait.

C 10. Why does Dorian go to his portrait while thingking of Hetty Merton?
- A. Dorian goes to pack the painting away so he can start over without the painting reminding him of his old ways.
- B. Dorain goes to destroy the painting.
- C. Dorian believes because he is trying to change the portrait will also change.
- D. Dorian goes to move the painting to another room in the house so he will never have to see it again.

FALSE FRIEND *The Picture of Dorian Gray*

by Susan R. Woodward

Must you hurt me again and again?
How will I ever know love if you constantly
Pull me in the wrong direction?
Oh, I thought I'd had it at times
But control, lust, anger and fear got in the way ...
Yeah, all that directed at me
As if I were an unappealing force to be reckoned with
And broken
While I stood there taking it
But not accepting it,
Trembling inside.

How could you let me get here this time?
What is it about you
That allows me to make these same mistakes?
I thought you were so smart ...

Pain so deep I can't cry it out;
Not enough tears to wash it away,
Hanging on a "maybe" as if it meant "yes"
Only to be disappointed again,
Crying myself to sleep.

Why can't anyone love me?
Or should I say "won't" 'cause love is a decision.
All deciding I'm not good enough
Either by walking away
Or else trying to change me.
Make me conform to their image of what I "ought" to be ...
Not someone to love as I am, huh?

Stop looking at me like that,
Like I should know better!
Maybe if you spoke up once in a while
My heart would be spared a trampling or two!

With a cry of frustration
I lash out in my hurt,
Propelling my fist full force into your face
Only to pick glass from bleeding knuckles.

READING COMPREHENSION QUESTIONS FOR "FALSE FRIEND" *The Picture of Dorian Gray*

Who is the "you" in the poem? Give at least three clues that provided a hint as to the false friend's identity.

Fully describe the images found in the poem. How do each of these images help to create an overall mood? Identify that mood.

Fully explain why the speaker must "pick glass from bleeding knuckles."

LESSON TWELVE

Objectives
1. To demonstrate cooperative learning skills by working in groups
2. To practice writing skills
3. To practice analytical skills through speculating about a character and writing about him/her
4. To practice analytical skills by answering discussion questions related to the novel

Activity 1
Give students time in this class period to work on writing the articles for their "newspapers" (Writing Assignment #2). Also, groups may choose to create paparazzi photos using a digital camera in the classroom.

Activity 2
(Homework)
Choose questions from the Extra Discussion Questions/Writing Assignments which seem most appropriate for your students. A class discussion of these questions is most effective if students have been given the opportunity to formulate answers to the questions prior to the discussion time. To this end, you may either have all the students formulate answers to all the questions, or assign one (or more) question(s) to each student in your class. The class discussion of these questions is scheduled for Lesson Fourteen.

Note: The use of graphic organizers may be helpful to students in preparing their answers. Encourage students to use any diagrams or graphics that they feel are necessary.

EXTRA DISCUSSION QUESTIONS/WRITING ASSIGNMENTS *The Picture of Dorian Gray*

Interpretive

1. Fully explain why Dorian murders Basil. What is it that he really wishes to kill?
2. Where is the climax of this novel? Explain your choice.
3. Explain how each of the following is partially responsible for the downfall of Dorian Gray: Basil Hallward, Lord Henry Wotton, Dorian himself.
4. What causes Dorian to make his rash wish? In your opinion, does he ever truly regret making the wish? Why or why not? How does granting of the wish have an impact on Dorian's character?
5. Why is Lord Henry Wotton also fascinated with Dorian Gray? What is Lord Henry's role in creating the main conflict of the novel? What does this demonstrate about his character?
6. Why is Basil Hallward so fascinated with young Dorian Gray when he first meets him? How does their relationship have an impact on Basil as an artist? What does this demonstrate about Basil's character?
7. Discuss three specific character traits for each of the following: Basil Hallward, Lord Henry Wotton, Dorian Gray, Sibyl Vane, Hames Vane, Sibyl Vane's mother, Alan Campbell, and Adrian Singleton.
8. What elements of setting are important to the Gothic novel? How would the novel have been different if it had been set in New York City? A tropical island? How would the setting have to be adjusted in order to maintain a Gothic quality?
9. How does the fact that the novel is set in Victorian England play an important part in the events of the plot? What elements of Victorian society play a key role in the main conflict?
10. What is the main conflict in *The Picture of Dorian Gray*?

Critical

11. Explain how the novel has an ironic ending.
12. Examine the following themes in *The Picture of Dorian Gray*. What message does Oscar Wilde seem to be sending his readers about each theme? (good vs. evil, the power of influence, the power of fear, the power of vanity)
13. For each of the following characters, select two objects (one specifically from the novel and one that is not) and explain how each object could be used to symbolize that person's particular trait's: Basil Hallward, Lord Henry Wotton, Dorian Gray, Sibyl Vane, James Vane, Alan Campbell, Sibyl Vane's mother, Adrian Singleton.
14. As a result of his marriage to the daughter of the Queen's Counsel, Oscar Wilde was able to live a life of relative luxury with much leisure time to devote to activities of pleasure. How does Wilde seem to fit the profile of a 19th century "dandy"? How is dandyism reflected in *The Picture of Dorian Gray*?
15. Oscar Wilde was a supporter of the Aesthetic movement in the 19th century. What is "aestheticism"? How is this idea presented in *The Picture of Dorian Gray*?
16. According to Carl Jung, each person has a shadow portion of his/her personality. This quality is often represented in literature as "doppelganger" or "dark twin." Explain why the idea of the doppelganger might attract readers of Gothic literature. How is that concept explored in Oscar Wilde's novel?
17. Fear is categorized as a negative emotion, yet many people seem to like to be scared. They seek thrill rides at amusement parks, go sky-diving, race cars, and watch horror movies. Those who read Gothic literature (especially horror literature) fall into a similar category of those who seem to like to be scared. What possible attraction might all of these activities draw for people?

18. Dramatic irony is when the reader is privy to specific information that the characters in the work do not have. How does Oscar Wilde use dramatic irony throughout *The Picture of Dorian Gray*? Why is it important that the reader knows the truth? How does the use of dramatic irony help create the atmosphere?
19. Does Lord Henry intentionally seek to spoil Dorian Gray through his negative influence? Explain your position using textual support as evidence.
20. How does the Gothic setting contribute to the overall mood or atmosphere of the novel? Give examples of how Oscar Wilde uses setting to create a specific atmosphere.

Critical/Personal Response

21. When Dorian tells Lord Henry that he killed Basil, Lord Henry doesn't believe him. Supposed that he did believe Dorian. What might have been the outcome?
22. Suppose that Dorian had not killed Basil in the upstairs room. What might have been the result of Basil's seeing the painting and being allowed to leave the house? How might he novel have changed?
23. What if Dorian had never met Lord Henry Wotton, yet he still made the wish regarding Basil's painting? Would the outcome of the novel had been the same? Explain.
24. Suppose that Dorian's rash wish had not come true. How might that have had an impact on his character? What events in the novel might have changed? What events may have stayed the same? Why?

Personal Response

25. Which of the characters do you identify with the most? Why?
26. Do you intend to read more books from the 19th Century Gothic genre? Why or why not?
27. What age do you think is most appropriate for reading novels like *The Picture of Dorian Gray*? Explain why.
28. Do you enjoy being scared? Why or why not? Did you think any parts of *The Picture of Dorian Gray* were scary? Why or why not?

LESSON THIRTEEN

Objectives
To review all the vocabulary work done in this unit on *The Picture of Dorian Gray*

Activity
Choose one (or more) of the vocabulary review activities listed below and spend your class time as directed. Some of the materials for these review activities are located in the vocabulary resource materials section of this LitPlan.

VOCABULARY REVIEW ACTIVITIES

1. Divide your class into two teams and have an old-fashioned spelling or definition bee.

2. Give each of your students (or students in groups of two, three or four) a *Picture of Dorian Gray* Vocabulary Word Search Puzzle. The person (group) to find all of the vocabulary words in the puzzle first wins.

3. Give students a *Picture of Dorian Gray* Vocabulary Word Search Puzzle without the word list. The person or group to find the most vocabulary words in the puzzle wins.

4. Use a *Picture of Dorian Gray* Vocabulary Crossword Puzzle. Put the puzzle onto a transparency on the overhead projector (so everyone can see it), and do the puzzle together as a class.

5. Give students a *Picture of Dorian Gray* Vocabulary Matching Worksheet to do.

6. Divide your class into two teams. Use *Picture of Dorian Gray* vocabulary words with their letters jumbled as a word list. Student 1 from Team A faces off against Student 1 from Team B. You write the first jumbled word on the board. The first student (1A or 1B) to unscramble the word wins the chance for his/her team to score points. If 1A wins the jumble, go to student 2A and give him/her a definition. He/she must give you the correct spelling of the vocabulary word which fits that definition. If he/she does, Team A scores a point, and you give student 3A a definition for which you expect a correctly spelled matching vocabulary word. Continue giving Team A definitions until some team member makes an incorrect response. An incorrect response sends the game back to the jumbled-word face off, this time with students 2A and 2B. Instead of repeating giving definitions to the first few students of each team, continue with the student after the one who gave the last incorrect response on the team. For example, if Team B wins the jumbled-word face-off, and student 5B gave the last incorrect answer for Team B, you would start this round of definition questions with student 6B, and so on. The team with the most points wins!

7. Have students write a story in which they correctly use as many vocabulary words as possible. Have students read their compositions orally! Post the most original compositions on your bulletin board!

8. Play I Have, Who Has? *NOTE this requires preparation in advance. On 3 x 5 cards, write a vocabulary word on one side and a definition to another word on the other side of the card. After you have completed a set, distribute the cards in a random order, keeping one for yourself. You will start the game by saying, "Who has [read the definition on your card]?" The student who has the word on his/her card that matches the definition shouts, "I Have [the word that matches your definition]!" He/she then turns his/her card over and says, "Who has [the definition on his/her card]?" and play continues until all the cards have been used.

9. Divide the class into two teams and play Baseball. The "pitcher" reads the definition of a word and in order to get a "hit," the "batter" must give the correct word to match the definition. For this game, though, only one strike is allowed! If the "batter" gives the correct word, he/she moves to first base and the next "batter" comes up for another word. Score is kept like baseball with three outs and the teams switching roles.

LESSON FOURTEEN

Objectives
1. To demonstrate an understanding of the novel beyond the factual questions asked in the study guide
2. To practice public speaking through giving oral answers to the discussion questions and participating in the class discussion

Activity

Use this class period to discuss the Extra Discussion Questions associated with the novel.

If you assigned specific questions to specific students, have each student lead a discussion about his/her question.

If you did not assign specific questions to specific students, hold your class discussion of these questions in whatever way you think is best for your situation.

LESSON FIFTEEN

Objectives
1. To demonstrate and practice writing skills through the completion of an in-class writing assignment
2. To demonstrate the ability to work independently
3. To practice writing to persuade

Activity 1
Distribute Writing Assignment #3 and discuss the directions in detail. Give students this whole class period to do the assignment.

NOTE:
Students who finish early could work on other writing assignments that have not yet been turned in (or have been returned for revisions), clean up study materials (study questions, vocabulary worksheets, class notes from discussions, etc.), or (if the study materials are already in good shape) review materials covered in class so far.

WRITING ASSIGNMENT #3 *The Picture of Dorian Gray*

PROMPT
You will read three quotations and select the one you feel best supports the main idea of Oscar Wilde's *The Picture of Dorian Gray*. In your essay, you need to indicate whether or not you agree with the main idea of the quotation and then defend your position by using specific textual support from *The Picture of Dorian Gray*.

PREWRITING
Choose one of the following quotes:

Purity of mind and idleness are incompatible.
  --*Mahatma Gandhi*

The body of a sensualist is the coffin of a dead soul.
  --*Christian Nestell Bovee*

We may have civilized bodies and yet barbarous souls.
  --*Herman Melville*

Decide whether or not you agree with the main idea of your selected quotation and choose specific textual evidence from *The Picture of Dorian Gray* that best supports your position.

DRAFTING
In your introduction, explain the meaning of the selected quotation and state whether or not you agree with the speaker (without using first person). This is best done by indicating whether or not the statement is true. At the end of your introduction, create a thesis statement in which you refer to Oscar Wilde's novel as support for your position. Your body paragraphs should contain at least two specific scenes from *The Picture of Dorian Gray* (complete with embedded quotations and parenthetical citations) that support your position of the quotation. Conclude your essay with some sort of a challenge to your reader with reference to the quotation.

PROMPT
When you finish the rough draft of your essay, set it aside and bring it to the next class for a peer-edit. After reading your rough draft, your editor will tell you what he/she liked best about your work, which parts were difficult to understand, and ways in which your work could be improved. Reread your essay considering your critic's comments, respond to the comments on the editing sheet, and make the corrections you think are necessary.

PROOFREADING
Do a final proofreading of your essay double-checking your grammar, spelling, organization, and the clarity of your ideas.

LESSON SIXTEEN

Objectives
1. To demonstrate students' ability to assess another's writing through a peer editing exercise
2. To demonstrate the ability to accept constructive criticism
3. To demonstrate the ability to determine which constructive criticism is best to heed (and which is not) by making necessary revisions to written work

Activity 1
Put students in pairs for peer editing and give each student a Peer Editing Form. Students will exchange their persuasive essays written in class the day before and make comments regarding the content, language use, and conventions (under "Editor"). Students will return the essays with the Peer Editing Forms to the writers and then the writers will respond to the Editors' comments (under "Writer"). After thanking their peers for their comments, students will revise and rewrite the essay as they feel is necessary.

Activity 2
If students finish the writing assignment early, they shoud work on finishing their projects for the upcoming presentations.

NOTE:
Remind students to bring in printed out copies of their completed articles for the next class. The groups will be putting together the "layout" of their newspapers.

Editor's Name _____ Date _____

Writer's Name _____ Assignment _____

Peer Editing for Writing Assignments

A. Was the writer's position clearly stated?

If your answer is "yes," be sure to tell the writer what he/she did that you especially liked. If your answer is "no," tell the writer what he/she could have included in order to write a better essay.

Editor: _____
_____
_____

Writer: _____
_____
_____

B. Did he/she provide enough details to support his/her position?

If your answer is "yes," be sure to tell the writer what you especially liked about his/her response. If your answer is "no," you must tell the writer how he/she could improve his/her response (adding specific details that were missed, connecting to position better, or adding embedded quotations).

Editor: _____
_____
_____

Writer: _____
_____
_____

C. Identify sentence type

Be sure to know the difference between simple, simple with compound subject, simple with compound predicate, compound, complex, and compound-complex. Using the first body paragraph, correctly identify each sentence type. If there is sufficient sentence structure variety, tell the writer what he/she did well. If not, explain what he/she could have done differently.

Sentence 1: _____   *Sentence 5:* _____

Sentence 2: _____   *Sentence 6:* _____

Sentence 3: _____   *Sentence 7:* _____

Sentence 4: _____   *Sentence 8:* _____

*Editor:*_____
_____
_____

*Writer:*_____
_____
_____

D. Address the Focus Correction Areas
Did the writer follow the specifics of the essay such as (address each individually):

Organization:

Editor: _____

Writer: _____

Use of Vocabulary as Directed:

Editor: _____

Writer: _____

Citations from novel as support:

Editor: _____

Writer: _____

E. Check for Errors in Punctuation, Grammar, Spelling, etc.

Editor: _____

Writer: _____

Comments:

LESSON SEVENTEEN

<u>Objectives</u>
1. To demonstrate the ability to work in cooperative groups
2. To create a layout/design for students' newspapers

<u>Activity</u>
Place students in their newspaper groups. Each group will design and complete its newspaper's layout. Remind students that each newspaper must have a catchy title and that both articles from each member of the group must appear in the newspaper.

Encourage students to be creative. In addition to the articles, they may include pictures, ads, etc. After students decide on a layout, they should create a "dummy" or mock-up of their newspaper. They could do this on posterboard (if you want to be able to post the presentations) or on regular paper to be copied and distributed for the presentations.

Remind each group to be ready to "present" their newspapers to the class in the next class period.

LESSONS EIGHTEEN AND NINETEEN

Objectives
1. To practice public speaking skills through the presentation of student-created newspapers
2. To practice listening skills by listening to the presentations of other students in the class
3. To demonstrate questioning skills through the formulation of a question and answer session about each article presented

Activity
Students will "sell" their papers and read articles from their newspapers. After an article has been read, audience members may question the writer about the incident being reported (like a press conference). Depending on the number of students you have and how much they "get into" the discussions after each article is read, this activity may take two class periods.

A group presentation evaluation form has been included in this unit for your convenience. You may choose to have students each complete one for each group (in addition to your completing one for each group).

NOTE:
If all groups finish with the presentations before the allotted time is over, students may choose study partners and quiz each other from the study questions, discussion questions, or vocabulary worksheets.

Group Presentation Evaluation Sheet

Each of the following will be graded on a scale of 1-5, with 1 being the lowest; each is worth 20% of the overall grade.

Part I: individual contribution during the preparation time in class (This has been monitored during in-class group work)
Part II: individual contribution to the group project/performance (how well he/she is prepared to read from his/her articles)
Part III: individual contributed to the correct format of the scandal sheet
Part IV: individual portion of the article remains true to the references in the novel
Part V: individual has provided all of his/her necessary portions of the group project (this includes the creation of two separate articles)

Name of Scandal Sheet:

Student Name	Part I	Part II	Part III	Part IV	Part V	Total Score

LESSON TWENTY

Objectives
To review the information covered in the *Picture of Dorian Gray* unit in preparation for the unit test

Activity
Choose one (or more) of the review activities below and use your class time accordingly.

Unit Review Activities

1. Ask the class to make up a unit test for *The Picture of Dorian Gray*. The test should have 4 sections: matching, true/false, short answer, and essay. Students may use 1/2 period to make the test and then swap papers and use the other 1/2 class period to take a test a classmate has devised. (open book) You may want to use the unit test included in this packet or take questions from the students' unit tests to formulate your own test.

2. Take 1/2 period for students to make up true and false questions (including the answers). Collect the papers and divide the class into two teams. Draw a big tic-tac-toe board on the chalk board. Make one team X and one team O. Ask questions to each side, giving each student one turn. If the question is answered correctly, that student's team's letter (X or O) is placed in the box. If the answer is incorrect, no letter is placed in the box. The object is to get three in a row like tic-tac-toe. You may want to keep track of the number of games won for each team.

3. Take 1/2 period for students to make up questions (true/false and short answer). Collect the questions. Divide the class into two teams. You'll alternate asking questions to individual members of teams A & B (like in a spelling bee). The question keeps going from A to B until it is correctly answered, then a new question is asked. A correct answer does not allow the team to get another question. Correct answers are +2 points; incorrect answers are -1 point.

4. Have students pair up and quiz each other from their study guides and class notes.

5. Give students a *Picture of Dorian Gray* crossword puzzle to complete.

6. Divide your class into two teams. Use *Picture of Dorian Gray* crossword words with their letters jumbled as a word list. Student 1 from Team A faces off against Student 1 from Team B. You write the first jumbled word on the board. The first student (1A or 1B) to unscramble the word wins the chance for his/her team to score points. If 1A wins the jumble, go to student 2A and give him/her a clue. He/she must give you the correct word which matches that clue. If he/she does, Team A scores a point, and you give student 3A a clue for which you expect another correct response. Continue giving Team A clues until some team member makes an incorrect response. An incorrect response sends the game back to the jumbled-word face off, this time with students 2A and 2B. Instead of repeating giving clues to the first few students of each team, continue with the student after the one who gave the last incorrect response on the team. For example, if Team B wins the jumbled-word face-off, and student 5B gave the last incorrect answer for Team B, you would start this round of clue questions with student 6B, and so on. The team with the most points wins!

7. Play What's My Line?. This is similar to the old television show. Students assume the roles of different characters from the novel. One student gives clues to the class, or to a panel of contestants. The contestants try to guess the identity of the guest. Students may enjoy assisting you in creating rules and procedures for the game.

8. Play Jeopardy. Divide the class into two groups. Assign each group a category or reading assignment from the novel and have them devise answers for that category. Play the game according to the television show procedures.

9. Play Drawing in the Details. This is similar to Pictionary. Divide students into teams. A student from one team draws a scene from the novel. (You may want to specify the section.) Drawings should be kept simple, to keep the pace lively. Students in the opposing team locate the scene in their books and read it aloud. If they are incorrect, the illustrator's team has a chance to guess. Involve students in setting up a scoring system and any other necessary rules.

10. Play I Have, Who Has? *NOTE This requires preparation in advance. On 3x5 cards, write a clue word on one side and a clue/definition/question to another clue word on the other side of the card. Once you have completed a set, pass that cards out randomly, keeping one for yourself. You will start the game by saying, "Who Has..." and reading the definition/question on the card. The student who has the answer on his/her card that matches the definition/question shouts, "I Have..." and reads the answer. He/She then turns over the card and says "Who Has..." and play continues until the all the cards have been gone through.

11. Divide the class into two teams and play Baseball. The "pitcher" reads a question about the novel and in order to get a "hit" the "batter" must correctly answer the question. For this game, though, only one strike is allowed! If the "batter" gives the correct answer, he/she moves to first base and the next "batter" comes up for another question. Score is kept like baseball with three outs and the teams switch places.

LESSON TWENTY-ONE

<u>Objectives</u>
To test students' understanding of the main ideas and themes presented in *The Picture of Dorian Gray*

<u>Activity</u>
Distribute the unit tests, give students ample time to complete them, and collect the tests when students finish. Remember to collect assigned books prior to the end of the class period.

NOTE: There are 5 different unit tests included in the LitPlan Teacher Pack. Two are short answer, two are multiple choice. There is one advanced short answer test. The answers to the advanced short answer test will be based on the discussions you have had during class and should be graded accordingly. You should choose the tests and/or test parts which best suit your needs. Matching and short answer tests have answer keys. For essay type questions, grade according to your own criteria based on class discussions and the level of your students. Also, you will need to choose vocabulary words to read orally for the vocabulary section of the short answer tests.

UNIT TESTS

The Picture of Dorian Gray SHORT ANSWER UNIT TEST 1

I. Matching

____ 1.	BASIL	A.	She commits suicide.
____ 2.	HENRY	B.	He disposes of Basil's body.
____ 3.	DORIAN	C.	Sibyl's theater role
____ 4.	FATHER	D.	He painted the portrait of Dorian Gray.
____ 5.	ERSKINE	E.	Lord Henry's wife
____ 6.	VICTORIA	F.	He wants to kill Dorian.
____ 7.	SYBIL	G.	Dorian's was killed in a duel.
____ 8.	JULIET	H.	He sees Dorian at the opium house.
____ 9.	ISAACS	I.	Author
____ 10.	DUCHESS	J.	She thinks living in the country is boring.
____ 11.	JAMES	K.	Person who asks Lord Henry how to become young again
____ 12.	LEAF	L.	Last name of Sibyl and James
____ 13.	BERWICK	M.	He murders Basil.
____ 14.	CAMPBELL	N.	He advances Sibyl's family 50 pounds.
____ 15.	NARBOROUGH	O.	He shoots the man hiding in the thicket.
____ 16.	SINGLETON	P.	He claims Lord Henry is extremely dangerous.
____ 17.	CLOUSTON	Q.	Young peasant girl Dorian chooses to leave while she is still pure
____ 18.	HETTY	R.	He had a negative influence on Dorian: Lord ___.
____ 19.	WILDE	S.	He leaves the smoking room when Dorian arrives.
____ 20.	VANE	T.	Dorian's housekeeper

II. Short Answer

1. Why doesn't Basil want to introduce Lord Henry to Dorian Gray?

2. According to Lord Henry, what is "the only way to get rid of a temptation"?

3. What does Dorian Gray so desperately wish for that he "would give [his] soul" to have it come true?

4. What news is in the telegram that Lord Henry receives from Dorian?

5. When Lord Henry and Basil accompany Dorian to the theatre, what happens to make Dorian angry?

6. After he breaks off his relationship with Sibyl, what does Dorian notice about the painting Basil had done of him?

7. What news is in Lord Henry's letter that Dorian does not open?

8. Who does Basil blame for the changes in Dorian?

9. Dorian threatens never to speak to Basil again. Why?

10. Where does Dorian Gray decide to hide the painting?

11. What does the coroner give as the official cause of Sibyl Vane's death?

12. What becomes a huge influence over Dorian Gray's life?

13. What does Dorian Gray do to Basil?

14. What does Dorian do to provide himself with an alibi regarding Basil's death?

15. What request does Dorian Gray make of Alan Campbell?

16. Why does Alan Campbell agree to do as Dorian asks?

17. What words did Lord Henry say the first day he met Dorian that now repeatedly play through Dorian's mind?

18. Why doesn't the drunken sailor shoot Dorian Gray?

19. Why does Dorian go to look at his portrait while thinking of Hetty Merton?

20. What happens to Dorian Gray?

III. Composition
1. What elements of setting are important to the Gothic novel? How would the novel have been different if it had been set in New York City? A tropical island? How would the setting have to be adjusted in order to maintain a Gothic quality?

2. Where is the climax of this novel? Explain your choice.

IV. Vocabulary
   A. Write the vocabulary words you are given. After writing them down, go back and write in their definitions.

Word	Definition
1	
2	
3	
4	
5	
6	
7	
8	
9	
10	

The Picture of Dorian Gray SHORT ANSWER UNIT TEST 1 Answer Key

I. Matching

D	1.	BASIL	A.	She commits suicide.
R	2.	HENRY	B.	He disposes of Basil's body.
M	3.	DORIAN	C.	Sibyl's theater role
G	4.	FATHER	D.	He painted the portrait of Dorian Gray.
P	5.	ERSKINE	E.	Lord Henry's wife
E	6.	VICTORIA	F.	He wants to kill Dorian.
A	7.	SYBIL	G.	Dorian's was killed in a duel.
C	8.	JULIET	H.	He sees Dorian at the opium house.
N	9.	ISAACS	I.	Author
K	10.	DUCHESS	J.	She thinks living in the country is boring.
F	11.	JAMES	K.	Person who asks Lord Henry how to become young again
T	12.	LEAF	L.	Last name of Sibyl and James
S	13.	BERWICK	M.	He murders Basil.
B	14.	CAMPBELL	N.	He advances Sibyl's family 50 pounds.
J	15.	NARBOROUGH	O.	He shoots the man hiding in the thicket.
H	16.	SINGLETON	P.	He claims Lord Henry is extremely dangerous.
O	17.	CLOUSTON	Q.	Young peasant girl Dorian chooses to leave while she is still pure
Q	18.	HETTY	R.	He had a negative influence on Dorian: Lord ___.
I	19.	WILDE	S.	He leaves the smoking room when Dorian arrives.
L	20.	VANE	T.	Dorian's housekeeper

II. Short Answer
1. Why doesn't Basil want to introduce Lord Henry to Dorian Gray?
   Basil is afraid that Lord Henry will be a negative influence on the young Dorian.
2. According to Lord Henry, what is "the only way to get rid of a temptation"?
   Lord Henry believes that "the only way to get rid of a temptation is to yield to it."
3. What does Dorian Gray so desperately wish for that he "would give [his] soul" to have it come true?
   Dorian wishes that his portrait would age and that he would remain young and untouched by the ugliness of life.
4. What news is in the telegram that Lord Henry receives from Dorian?
   Dorian sends a telegram to Lord Henry announcing his engagement to Sibyl Vane.
5. When Lord Henry and Basil accompany Dorian to the theatre, what happens to make Dorian angry?
   Sibyl's performance is terrible. Lord Henry and Basil leave during the show.
6. After he breaks off his relationship with Sibyl, what does Dorian notice about the painting Basil had done of him?
   The painting has changed, and on the face of the painting "there was a touch of cruelty in the mouth."
7. What news is in Lord Henry's letter that Dorian does not open?
   Lord Henry's note says he has learned that Sibyl Vane died in an incident at the theater.
8. Who does Basil blame for the changes in Dorian?
   Basil blames Lord Henry for the negative changes in Dorian.
9. Dorian threatens never to speak to Basil again. Why?
   Dorian doesn't want Basil to see the painting, so he threatens never to speak to Basil again if Basil looks at it.
10. Where does Dorian Gray decide to hide the painting?
    Dorian decides to move the painting into an old schoolroom at the top of his house and keep the painting under lock and key.
11. What does the coroner give as the official cause of Sibyl Vane's death?
    The coroner's official report is that Sibyl Vane met her "death by misadventure." It was officially proclaimed an accidental death.
12. What becomes a huge influence over Dorian Gray's life?
    The book that Lord Henry gave Dorian has a huge influence over Dorian's behavior. He is so caught up in it, he purchases nine copies of it and has them bound in various colors to match his changing moods.
13. What does Dorian Gray do to Basil?
    Dorian viciously stabs Basil in the neck with an artist's knife.
14. What does Dorian do to provide himself with an alibi regarding Basil's death?
    Dorian goes outside and bangs on his door to awaken his servants. In doing so his servants will provide him with an alibi that he returned home after Basil had gone.
15. What request does Dorian Gray make of Alan Campbell?
    Dorian asks Alan Campbell to dispose of Basil's body through the use of chemicals and fire.
16. Why does Alan Campbell agree to do as Dorian asks?
    Dorian Gray blackmails Alan Campbell with some deed from his past when he and Dorian had been friends. Dorian threatens to ruin Alan's reputation if he doesn't do it.

17. What words did Lord Henry say the first day he met Dorian that now repeatedly play through Dorian's mind?
    On the day they had met, Lord Henry told Dorian that one could "cure the soul by means of the senses and the senses by means of the soul."
18. Why doesn't the drunken sailor shoot Dorian Gray?
    Dorian tells James to look at him closely under a street lamp and see that, with his youthful looks, he could not have possibly been the man who caused Sibyl Vane to commit suicide eighteen years earlier.
19. Why does Dorian go to look at his portrait while thinking of Hetty Merton?
    Dorian believes that the picture must now be shedding its ugliness since he has decided to become good, and he had committed a "good deed" by leaving Hetty.
20. What happens to Dorian Gray?
    Dorian attempts to destroy the painting by stabbing it. However, when the servants break into the room (after hearing a loud cry of anguish), they find an old decrepit man with a knife in his heart next to a beautiful painting of Dorian Gray. They only recognize the dead man as their master when they see his rings."

IV. Vocabulary
   Write the vocabulary words and definitions you will use for this test.

Word	Definition
1	
2	
3	
4	
5	
6	
7	
8	
9	
10	

The Picture of Dorian Gray SHORT ANSWER UNIT TEST 2

I. Matching

____ 1. BASIL   A. Person who asks Lord Henry how to become young again
____ 2. HENRY   B. Dorian's housekeeper
____ 3. DORIAN   C. Last name of Sibyl and James
____ 4. FATHER   D. Author
____ 5. ERSKINE   E. He leaves the smoking room when Dorian arrives.
____ 6. VICTORIA   F. Lord Henry's wife
____ 7. SYBIL   G. She commits suicide.
____ 8. JULIET   H. He had a negative influence on Dorian: Lord ___.
____ 9. ISAACS   I. He wants to kill Dorian.
____ 10. DUCHESS   J. He sees Dorian at the opium house.
____ 11. JAMES   K. Sibyl's theater role
____ 12. LEAF   L. He claims Lord Henry is extremely dangerous.
____ 13. BERWICK   M. He advances Sibyl's family 50 pounds.
____ 14. CAMPBELL   N. He shoots the man hiding in the thicket.
____ 15. NARBOROUGH   O. Young peasant girl Dorian chooses to leave while she is still pure
____ 16. SINGLETON   P. She thinks living in the country is boring.
____ 17. CLOUSTON   Q. He disposes of Basil's body.
____ 18. HETTY   R. He murders Basil.
____ 19. WILDE   S. He painted the portrait of Dorian Gray.
____ 20. VANE   T. Dorian's was killed in a duel.

II. Short Answer

1. Why doesn't Basil want to introduce Lord Henry to Dorian Gray?

2. What does Dorian Gray so desperately wish for that he "would give [his] soul" to have it come true?

3. What news is in the telegram that Lord Henry receives from Dorian?

4. What does it mean to be "good," according to Lord Henry?

5. After he breaks off his relationship with Sibyl, what does Dorian notice about the painting Basil had done of him?

6. What news is in Lord Henry's letter that Dorian does not open?

7. Who does Basil blame for the changes in Dorian?

8. Why do people tend to disbelieve the rumors about Dorian Gray?

9. What are some of the activities or interests that capture Dorian Gray's attention in his study of the senses?

10. What sort of fate have many of Dorian's acquaintances met?

11. What does Basil claim that he would have to see before he could believe anything he's heard about Dorian's activities?

12. What does Basil implore Dorian to do after seeing the condition of the painting?

13. What does Dorian Gray do to Basil?

14. What request does Dorian Gray make of Alan Campbell?

15. Whom does Lady Narbourough accuse of being "extremely wicked"?

16. Who is the drunken sailor who accuses Dorian Gray in the street?

17. What does Dorian Gray blame for raising "such fearful phantoms" that keep him in his house for three days?

18. What does Dorian claim is "a terrible reality . . . [that] . . . can be bought, and sold, and bartered away"?

19. Why does Dorian go to look at his portrait while thinking of Hetty Merton?

20. What happens to Dorian Gray?

III. Composition
1. Why is Lord Henry Wotton also fascinated with Dorian Gray? What is Lord Henry's role in creating the main conflict of the novel? What does this demonstrate about his character?

2. Where is the climax of this novel? Explain your choice.

IV. Vocabulary
    A. Write the vocabulary words you are given. After writing them down, go back and write in their definitions.

Word	Definition
1	
2	
3	
4	
5	
6	
7	
8	
9	
10	

The Picture of Dorian Gray SHORT ANSWER UNIT TEST 2 Answer Key

I. Matching

S	1.	BASIL	A.	Person who asks Lord Henry how to become young again
H	2.	HENRY	B.	Dorian's housekeeper
R	3.	DORIAN	C.	Last name of Sibyl and James
T	4.	FATHER	D.	Author
L	5.	ERSKINE	E.	He leaves the smoking room when Dorian arrives.
F	6.	VICTORIA	F.	Lord Henry's wife
G	7.	SYBIL	G.	She commits suicide.
K	8.	JULIET	H.	He had a negative influence on Dorian: Lord ___.
M	9.	ISAACS	I.	He wants to kill Dorian.
A	10.	DUCHESS	J.	He sees Dorian at the opium house.
I	11.	JAMES	K.	Sibyl's theater role
B	12.	LEAF	L.	He claims Lord Henry is extremely dangerous.
E	13.	BERWICK	M.	He advances Sibyl's family 50 pounds.
Q	14.	CAMPBELL	N.	He shoots the man hiding in the thicket.
P	15.	NARBOROUGH	O.	Young peasant girl Dorian chooses to leave while she is still pure
J	16.	SINGLETON	P.	She thinks living in the country is boring.
N	17.	CLOUSTON	Q.	He disposes of Basil's body.
O	18.	HETTY	R.	He murders Basil.
D	19.	WILDE	S.	He painted the portrait of Dorian Gray.
C	20.	VANE	T.	Dorian's was killed in a duel.

II. Short Answer

1. Why doesn't Basil want to introduce Lord Henry to Dorian Gray?
   Basil is afraid that Lord Henry will be a negative influence on the young Dorian.

2. What does Dorian Gray so desperately wish for that he "would give [his] soul" to have it come true?
   Dorian wishes that his portrait would age and that he would remain young and untouched by the ugliness of life.

3. What news is in the telegram that Lord Henry receives from Dorian?
   Dorian sends a telegram to Lord Henry announcing his engagement to Sibyl Vane.

4. What does it mean to be "good," according to Lord Henry?
   To be good is to be in harmony with oneself.

5. After he breaks off his relationship with Sibyl, what does Dorian notice about the painting Basil had done of him?
   The painting has changed, and on the face of the painting "there was a touch of cruelty in the mouth."

6. What news is in Lord Henry's letter that Dorian does not open?
   Lord Henry's note says he has learned that Sibyl Vane died in an incident at the theater.

7. Who does Basil blame for the changes in Dorian?
   Basil blames Lord Henry for the negative changes in Dorian.

8. Why do people tend to disbelieve the rumors about Dorian Gray?
   Because the portrait in his upstairs room absorbed all the aging and marks of sin, Dorian's youthful beauty keeps people from believing the worst about him.

9. What are some of the activities or interests that capture Dorian Gray's attention in his study of the senses?
   Dorian, over a period of several years, delves into many areas of interest. Dorian studies embroidered clothing, tapestries, jewels, perfumes, the ritual of Roman Catholicism, mysticism, and music. When he gets bored with one topic, he moves on to the next.

10. What sort of fate have many of Dorian's acquaintances met?
    Those who were closest to Dorian have lost their respectable reputations in society.

11. What does Basil claim that he would have to see before he could believe anything he's heard about Dorian's activities?
    Basil claims that he would have to see Dorian's soul before he could believe any of the rumors he's heard about Dorian.

12. What does Basil implore Dorian to do after seeing the condition of the painting?
    Basil begs Dorian to get on his knees and pray to God for forgiveness of his sins.

13. What does Dorian Gray do to Basil?
    Dorian viciously stabs Basil in the neck with an artist's knife.

14. What request does Dorian Gray make of Alan Campbell?
    Dorian asks Alan Campbell to dispose of Basil's body through the use of chemicals and fire.

15. Whom does Lady Narbourough accuse of being "extremely wicked"?
    Lady Narborough accuses Lord Henry of being extremely wicked.

16. Who is the drunken sailor who accuses Dorian Gray in the street?
    The drunken sailor is James Vane, Sibyl Vane's older brother, who had vowed to kill "Prince Charming" if he ever hurt his sister.

17. What does Dorian Gray blame for raising "such fearful phantoms" that keep him in his house for three days?
He blames his conscience.

18. What does Dorian claim is "a terrible reality . . . [that] . . . can be bought, and sold, and bartered away"?
Dorian says this about the soul.

19. Why does Dorian go to look at his portrait while thinking of Hetty Merton?
Dorian believes that the picture must now be shedding its ugliness since he has decided to become good, and he had committed a "good deed" by leaving Hetty.

20. What happens to Dorian Gray?
Dorian attempts to destroy the painting by stabbing it. However, when the servants break into the room (after hearing a loud cry of anguish), they find an old decrepit man with a knife in his heart next to a beautiful painting of Dorian Gray. They only recognize the dead man as their master when they see his rings."

IV. Vocabulary
   Write the vocabulary words and definitions you will use for this test.

Word	Definition
1	
2	
3	
4	
5	
6	
7	
8	
9	
10	

The Picture of Dorian Gray ADVANCED SHORT ANSWER TEST

I. Matching

____ 1. BASIL   A. Person who asks Lord Henry how to become young again
____ 2. HENRY   B. He sees Dorian at the opium house.
____ 3. DORIAN   C. He shoots the man hiding in the thicket.
____ 4. FATHER   D. He leaves the smoking room when Dorian arrives.
____ 5. ERSKINE   E. Dorian's housekeeper
____ 6. VICTORIA   F. He claims Lord Henry is extremely dangerous.
____ 7. SYBIL   G. He painted the portrait of Dorian Gray.
____ 8. JULIET   H. He murders Basil.
____ 9. ISAACS   I. Young peasant girl Dorian chooses to leave while she is still pure
____ 10. DUCHESS   J. He wants to kill Dorian.
____ 11. JAMES   K. He had a negative influence on Dorian: Lord ___.
____ 12. LEAF   L. He advances Sibyl's family 50 pounds.
____ 13. BERWICK   M. Lord Henry's wife
____ 14. CAMPBELL   N. He disposes of Basil's body.
____ 15. NARBOROUGH   O. Last name of Sibyl and James
____ 16. SINGLETON   P. Dorian's was killed in a duel.
____ 17. CLOUSTON   Q. Sibyl's theater role
____ 18. HETTY   R. She thinks living in the country is boring.
____ 19. WILDE   S. Author
____ 20. VANE   T. She commits suicide.

II. Short Answer
1. What is the main conflict in *The Picture of Dorian Gray*?

2. How does the fact that the novel is set in Victorian England play an important part in the events of the plot? What elements of Victorian society play a key role in the main conflict?

3. What elements of setting are important to the Gothic novel? How would the novel have been different if it had been set in New York City? A tropical island? How would the setting have to be adjusted in order to maintain a Gothic quality?

4. Discuss three specific character traits for each of the following: Basil Hallward, Lord Henry Wotton, Dorian Gray, Sibyl Vane, Hames Vane, Sibyl Vane's mother, Alan Campbell, and Adrian Singleton.

5. Why is Basil Hallward so fascinated with young Dorian Gray when he first meets him? How does their relationship have an impact on Basil as an artist? What does this demonstrate about Basil's character?

6. Why is Lord Henry Wotton also fascinated with Dorian Gray? What is Lord Henry's role in creating the main conflict of the novel? What does this demonstrate about his character?

7. What causes Dorian to make his rash wish? In your opinion, does he ever truly regret making the wish? Why or why not? How does granting of the wish have an impact on Dorian's character?

8. Explain how each of the following is partially responsible for the downfall of Dorian Gray: Basil Hallward, Lord Henry Wotton, Dorian himself.

9. Where is the climax of this novel? Explain your choice.

10. Fully explain why Dorian murders Basil. What is it that he really wishes to kill?

III. Composition
1. Dramatic irony is when the reader is privy to specific information that the characters in the work do not have. How does Oscar Wilde use dramatic irony throughout *The Picture of Dorian Gray*? Why is it important that the reader knows the truth? How does the use of dramatic irony help create the atmosphere?

2. Examine the following themes in *The Picture of Dorian Gray*. What message does Oscar Wilde seem to be sending his readers about each theme? (good vs. evil, the power of influence, the power of fear, the power of vanity)

IV. Vocabulary
   A. Write the vocabulary words you are given. After writing them down, go back and write in their definitions.

Word	Definition
1	
2	
3	
4	
5	
6	
7	
8	
9	
10	

   B. Write a paragraph about the book using 8 of the 10 vocabulary words above.

The Picture of Dorian Gray ADVANCED SHORT ANSWER TEST Answer Key

I. Matching

G	1.	BASIL	A.	Person who asks Lord Henry how to become young again
K	2.	HENRY	B.	He sees Dorian at the opium house.
H	3.	DORIAN	C.	He shoots the man hiding in the thicket.
P	4.	FATHER	D.	He leaves the smoking room when Dorian arrives.
F	5.	ERSKINE	E.	Dorian's housekeeper
M	6.	VICTORIA	F.	He claims Lord Henry is extremely dangerous.
T	7.	SYBIL	G.	He painted the portrait of Dorian Gray.
Q	8.	JULIET	H.	He murders Basil.
L	9.	ISAACS	I.	Young peasant girl Dorian chooses to leave while she is still pure
A	10.	DUCHESS	J.	He wants to kill Dorian.
J	11.	JAMES	K.	He had a negative influence on Dorian: Lord ____.
E	12.	LEAF	L.	He advances Sibyl's family 50 pounds.
D	13.	BERWICK	M.	Lord Henry's wife
N	14.	CAMPBELL	N.	He disposes of Basil's body.
R	15.	NARBOROUGH	O.	Last name of Sibyl and James
B	16.	SINGLETON	P.	Dorian's was killed in a duel.
C	17.	CLOUSTON	Q.	Sibyl's theater role
I	18.	HETTY	R.	She thinks living in the country is boring.
S	19.	WILDE	S.	Author
O	20.	VANE	T.	She commits suicide.

IV. Vocabulary
    Write the vocabulary words and definitions you will use for this test.

Word	Definition
1	
2	
3	
4	
5	
6	
7	
8	
9	
10	

The Picture of Dorian Gray MULTIPLE CHOICE UNIT TEST 1

I. Matching

____ 1. BASIL   A. Sibyl's theater role
____ 2. HENRY   B. He disposes of Basil's body.
____ 3. DORIAN   C. He claims Lord Henry is extremely dangerous.
____ 4. FATHER   D. He advances Sibyl's family 50 pounds.
____ 5. ERSKINE   E. Dorian's was killed in a duel.
____ 6. VICTORIA   F. Lord Henry's wife
____ 7. SYBIL   G. Author
____ 8. JULIET   H. He shoots the man hiding in the thicket.
____ 9. ISAACS   I. Person who asks Lord Henry how to become young again
____ 10. DUCHESS   J. Last name of Sibyl and James
____ 11. JAMES   K. He wants to kill Dorian.
____ 12. LEAF   L. He had a negative influence on Dorian: Lord ___.
____ 13. BERWICK   M. He painted the portrait of Dorian Gray.
____ 14. CAMPBELL   N. Young peasant girl Dorian chooses to leave while she is still pure
____ 15. NARBOROUGH   O. He leaves the smoking room when Dorian arrives.
____ 16. SINGLETON   P. He murders Basil.
____ 17. CLOUSTON   Q. He sees Dorian at the opium house.
____ 18. HETTY   R. Dorian's housekeeper
____ 19. WILDE   S. She commits suicide.
____ 20. VANE   T. She thinks living in the country is boring.

II. Multiple Choice

1. Why doesn't Basil want to introduce Lord Henry to Dorian Gray?
   A. Basil is afraid that Lord Henry will be a negative influence on the young Dorian.
   B. Lord Henry is an evil old man who would ruin Dorian's reputation.
   C. Basil is afraid for Dorian's safety.
   D. Lord Henry is a known thief, and Basil wants to protect Dorian from involvement.

2. What becomes a huge influence over Dorian Gray's life?
   A. Dorian is fascinated with the way the painting changed; he just sits and watches it.
   B. The book that Lord Henry gave Dorian has a huge influence over Dorian's behavior.
   C. Dorian has a secret relationship with the Duchess for several years.
   D. Dorian has a torrid affair with Lord Henry's wife.

3. What does Dorian Gray do to Basil?
   A. Dorian shoves Basil out of the room, and Basil accidentally falls down the stairs and breaks his neck.
   B. Dorian viciously stabs Basil in the neck with an artist's knife.
   C. Dorian tells Basil to leave and never return.
   D. Dorian breaks down in tears and prays for Basil's forgiveness.

4. What does Dorian do to provide himself with an alibi regarding Basil's death?
   A. Dorian goes to the club and pretends to be upset because Basil has not joined him as planned.
   B. Dorian goes outside and bangs on his door to awaken his servants. In doing so his servants will provide him with an alibi that he returned home after Basil had gone.
   C. Dorian goes to the local brothel and pays one of the women to say he had been with her all night.
   D. Dorian goes to Lord Henry and asks him to provide Dorian with an alibi.

5. What request does Dorian Gray make of Alan Campbell?
   A. Dorian asks Alan Campbell to dispose of Basil's body.
   B. Dorian wants Alan to accompany him to Paris and pretend to be Basil Hallward.
   C. Dorian wants Alan to claim responsibility for Basil's death.
   D. Dorian wants Alan to pose as Basil for several days around London so that people will think that Basil is still alive; meanwhile, Dorian will go to Paris, creating an alibi.

6. Why does Alan Campbell agree to do as Dorian asks?
    A. Dorian blackmails Alan Campbell with some deed from his past.
    B. Alan feels sorry for Dorian and wishes to help him.
    C. Dorian pays Alan a huge amount of money to do as he asks.
    D. Alan knows that it is the only way to get Dorian Gray out of his life forever.

7. What words did Lord Henry say the first day he met Dorian that now repeatedly play through Dorian's mind?
    A. Lord Henry told Dorian that one could cure the soul by means of the senses and the senses by means of the soul.
    B. Lord Henry told Dorian that the painting truly is a reflection of Dorian's very soul.
    C. Lord Henry told Dorian that there is nothing to fear but fear itself.
    D. Lord Henry told Dorian that one could cure the soul by confessing their sins and changing their evil ways.

8. Why doesn't the drunken sailor shoot Dorian Gray?
    A. Dorian looks to young to be the man who caused Sibyl Vane to commit suicide.
    B. Dorian looks to old to be the man who caused Sibyl Vane to commit suicide.
    C. Lord Henry takes the gun away from the sailor before he has a change to shoot Dorian.
    D. Dorian disarms the sailor and takes him to the police.

9. Why does Dorian go to his portrait while thinking of Hetty Merton?
    A. Dorian believes because he is trying to change the portrait will also change.
    B. Dorain goes to destroy the painting.
    C. Dorian goes to move the painting to another room in the house so he will never have to see it again.
    D. Dorian goes to pack the painting away so he can start over without the painting reminding him of his old ways.

10. What does the coroner give as the official cause of Sibyl Vane's death?
    A. It was officially proclaimed a suicide.
    B. It was officially proclaimed death by natural causes.
    C. It was officially proclaimed an accidental death.
    D. It was officially proclaimed a murder.

11. Where does Dorian Gray decide to hide the painting?
    A. He hides it in the basement.
    B. He hides the painting in an old schoolroom at the top of his house.
    C. He hides it in a secret room behind the drawing room wainscoting.
    D. He hides it under his bed.

12. According to Lord Henry, what is "the only way to get rid of a temptation"?
    A. Lord Henry believes that the only way to get rid of a temptation is to yield to it.
    B. Lord Henry believes honest work will keep a man from temptation.
    C. Lord Henry believes one must pray earnestly to God to rid oneself of temptation.
    D. Lord Henry believes keeping a busy mind will keep the body from giving in to temptation.

13. What does Dorian Gray so desperately wish for that he "would give [his] soul" to have it come true?
    A. Dorian wishes for enough riches so that he will never have to work.
    B. Dorian wishes that his portrait would age while he remains young and untouched by the ugliness of life.
    C. Dorian wishes to meet and marry his soul mate.
    D. Dorian wishes that he could travel to America to study the Transcendentalists.

14. What news is in the telegram that Lord Henry receives from Dorian?
    A. Lord Henry's wife sends him a telegram informing him that she has run away with Dorian.
    B. Basil sends Lord Henry a telegram letting him know that Dorian has agreed to let Basil see the painting.
    C. Basil sends a telegram to Lord Henry informing him that Dorian has been injured in a terrible accident.
    D. Dorian sends a telegram to Lord Henry announcing his engagement to Sibyl Vane.

15. When Lord Henry and Basil accompany Dorian to the theatre, what happens to make Dorian angry?
    A. They are late arriving from dinner and are not allowed to enter during the show.
    B. Sibyl is so convincing as Juliet that Dorian has become jealous of "Romeo."
    C. Sibyl's performance is terrible. Lord Henry and Basil leave during the show.
    D. That night's performance has been cancelled.

16. After he breaks off his relationship with Sibyl, what does Dorian notice about the painting Basil had done of him?
    A. The painting has changed, and on the face of the painting there are tears in the eyes.
    B. The painting has changed, and on the face of the painting there was a touch of cruelty in the mouth.
    C. A black mold is beginning to form around the lower corners of the painting.
    D. Someone has tampered with the painting and marred its appearance.

17. What news is in Lord Henry's letter that Dorian does not open?
    A. Basil Hallward is missing.
    B. Lord Henry's wife has asked for a divorce and is leaving him.
    C. The Duchess is so angry with Dorian for standing her up that she vowed to ruin his reputation.
    D. Lord Henry's note says he has learned that Sibyl Vane died in an incident at the theater.

18. Who does Basil blame for the changes in Dorian?
    A. Himself
    B. Lord Henry
    C. Sibyl Vane
    D. The Duchess

19. Dorian threatens never to speak to Basil again. Why?
    A. Basil blames Dorian for Sibyl's death and wants Dorian to repent his sins.
    B. Basil wants to tell Lord Henry to stay away from Dorian.
    C. Dorian doesn't want Basil to see the painting, so he threatens never to speak to Basil again if Basil looks at it.
    D. Basil threatens to tell Dorian's grandfather about the difficulties Dorian is going through.

20. What happens to Dorian Gray?
    A. Dorian is arrested for the murder of Basil Hallward and is hanged.
    B. Dorian is killed by Lord Henry when Henry sees the painting.
    C. Dorian dies while trying to destroy the portrait.
    D. Dorian accidentally falls on the knife that he used to kill Basil.

III. Composition
1. What elements of setting are important to the Gothic novel? How would the novel have been different if it had been set in New York City? A tropical island? How would the setting have to be adjusted in order to maintain a Gothic quality?

2. Where is the climax of this novel? Explain your choice.

IV. Vocabulary

____ 1. ENSCONCED   A. Having an offensive odor; stinking
____ 2. MALADIES   B. Filthy or dirty; foul
____ 3. UNCOUTH   C. Area overgrown with ferns and shrubs
____ 4. ENTREAT   D. Feeling abandoned; forlorn
____ 5. PROTEGE   E. Fill with water and sink
____ 6. SORDID   F. Diminished or became tainted
____ 7. DESOLATE   G. To ask (a person) earnestly; beseech; implore
____ 8. INVARIABLY   H. Person who promotes or holds religious revivals
____ 9. HANSOM   I. Awkward, clumsy, or unmannerly
____ 10. IMPASSIVE   J. Greenhouse, usually attached to a dwelling
____ 11. CENSURE   K. Criticize or reproach harshly
____ 12. TARNISHED   L. Two-wheeled covered carriage with the driver's seat above and behind
____ 13. PARODY   M. Imitate for purposes of ridicule or satire
____ 14. FETID   N. Without emotion; apathetic; unmoved
____ 15. CONSERVATORY   O. Undesirable conditions or disorders
____ 16. ABDICATE   P. Settled securely or snugly
____ 17. FOUNDER   Q. Strike down, injure, or slay
____ 18. BRACKEN   R. Without variation or change, in every case
____ 19. REVIVALIST   S. One whose welfare is promoted by an influential person
____ 20. SMITE   T. Renounce or relinquish a throne, right, or power

The Picture of Dorian Gray MULTIPLE CHOICE UNIT TEST 1 Answer Key

I. Matching

M	1.	BASIL	A.	Sibyl's theater role
L	2.	HENRY	B.	He disposes of Basil's body.
P	3.	DORIAN	C.	He claims Lord Henry is extremely dangerous.
E	4.	FATHER	D.	He advances Sibyl's family 50 pounds.
C	5.	ERSKINE	E.	Dorian's was killed in a duel.
F	6.	VICTORIA	F.	Lord Henry's wife
S	7.	SYBIL	G.	Author
A	8.	JULIET	H.	He shoots the man hiding in the thicket.
D	9.	ISAACS	I.	Person who asks Lord Henry how to become young again
I	10.	DUCHESS	J.	Last name of Sibyl and James
K	11.	JAMES	K.	He wants to kill Dorian.
R	12.	LEAF	L.	He had a negative influence on Dorian: Lord ____.
O	13.	BERWICK	M.	He painted the portrait of Dorian Gray.
B	14.	CAMPBELL	N.	Young peasant girl Dorian chooses to leave while she is still pure
T	15.	NARBOROUGH	O.	He leaves the smoking room when Dorian arrives.
Q	16.	SINGLETON	P.	He murders Basil.
H	17.	CLOUSTON	Q.	He sees Dorian at the opium house.
N	18.	HETTY	R.	Dorian's housekeeper
G	19.	WILDE	S.	She commits suicide.
J	20.	VANE	T.	She thinks living in the country is boring.

II. Multiple Choice

A 1.   Why doesn't Basil want to introduce Lord Henry to Dorian Gray?
   A. Basil is afraid that Lord Henry will be a negative influence on the young Dorian.
   B. Lord Henry is an evil old man who would ruin Dorian's reputation.
   C. Basil is afraid for Dorian's safety.
   D. Lord Henry is a known thief, and Basil wants to protect Dorian from involvement.

B 2.   What becomes a huge influence over Dorian Gray's life?
   A. Dorian is fascinated with the way the painting changed; he just sits and watches it.
   B. The book that Lord Henry gave Dorian has a huge influence over Dorian's behavior.
   C. Dorian has a secret relationship with the Duchess for several years.
   D. Dorian has a torrid affair with Lord Henry's wife.

B 3.   What does Dorian Gray do to Basil?
   A. Dorian shoves Basil out of the room, and Basil accidentally falls down the stairs and breaks his neck.
   B. Dorian viciously stabs Basil in the neck with an artist's knife.
   C. Dorian tells Basil to leave and never return.
   D. Dorian breaks down in tears and prays for Basil's forgiveness.

B 4.   What does Dorian do to provide himself with an alibi regarding Basil's death?
   A. Dorian goes to the club and pretends to be upset because Basil has not joined him as planned.
   B. Dorian goes outside and bangs on his door to awaken his servants. In doing so his servants will provide him with an alibi that he returned home after Basil had gone.
   C. Dorian goes to the local brothel and pays one of the women to say he had been with her all night.
   D. Dorian goes to Lord Henry and asks him to provide Dorian with an alibi.

A 5.   What request does Dorian Gray make of Alan Campbell?
   A. Dorian asks Alan Campbell to dispose of Basil's body.
   B. Dorian wants Alan to accompany him to Paris and pretend to be Basil Hallward.
   C. Dorian wants Alan to claim responsibility for Basil's death.
   D. Dorian wants Alan to pose as Basil for several days around London so that people will think that Basil is still alive; meanwhile, Dorian will go to Paris, creating an alibi.

A 6. Why does Alan Campbell agree to do as Dorian asks?
  A. Dorian blackmails Alan Campbell with some deed from his past.
  B. Alan feels sorry for Dorian and wishes to help him.
  C. Dorian pays Alan a huge amount of money to do as he asks.
  D. Alan knows that it is the only way to get Dorian Gray out of his life forever.

A 7. What words did Lord Henry say the first day he met Dorian that now repeatedly play through Dorian's mind?
  A. Lord Henry told Dorian that one could cure the soul by means of the senses and the senses by means of the soul.
  B. Lord Henry told Dorian that the painting truly is a reflection of Dorian's very soul.
  C. Lord Henry told Dorian that there is nothing to fear but fear itself.
  D. Lord Henry told Dorian that one could cure the soul by confessing their sins and changing their evil ways.

A 8. Why doesn't the drunken sailor shoot Dorian Gray?
  A. Dorian looks to young to be the man who caused Sibyl Vane to commit suicide.
  B. Dorian looks to old to be the man who caused Sibyl Vane to commit suicide.
  C. Lord Henry takes the gun away from the sailor before he has a change to shoot Dorian.
  D. Dorian disarms the sailor and takes him to the police.

A 9. Why does Dorian go to his portrait while thinking of Hetty Merton?
  A. Dorian believes because he is trying to change the portrait will also change.
  B. Dorain goes to destroy the painting.
  C. Dorian goes to move the painting to another room in the house so he will never have to see it again.
  D. Dorian goes to pack the painting away so he can start over without the painting reminding him of his old ways.

C 10. What does the coroner give as the official cause of Sibyl Vane's death?
  A. It was officially proclaimed a suicide.
  B. It was officially proclaimed death by natural causes.
  C. It was officially proclaimed an accidental death.
  D. It was officially proclaimed a murder.

B 11. Where does Dorian Gray decide to hide the painting?
- A. He hides it in the basement.
- B. He hides the painting in an old schoolroom at the top of his house.
- C. He hides it in a secret room behind the drawing room wainscoting.
- D. He hides it under his bed.

A 12. According to Lord Henry, what is "the only way to get rid of a temptation"?
- A. Lord Henry believes that the only way to get rid of a temptation is to yield to it.
- B. Lord Henry believes honest work will keep a man from temptation.
- C. Lord Henry believes one must pray earnestly to God to rid oneself of temptation.
- D. Lord Henry believes keeping a busy mind will keep the body from giving in to temptation.

B 13. What does Dorian Gray so desperately wish for that he "would give [his] soul" to have it come true?
- A. Dorian wishes for enough riches so that he will never have to work.
- B. Dorian wishes that his portrait would age while he remains young and untouched by the ugliness of life.
- C. Dorian wishes to meet and marry his soul mate.
- D. Dorian wishes that he could travel to America to study the Transcendentalists.

D 14. What news is in the telegram that Lord Henry receives from Dorian?
- A. Lord Henry's wife sends him a telegram informing him that she has run away with Dorian.
- B. Basil sends Lord Henry a telegram letting him know that Dorian has agreed to let Basil see the painting.
- C. Basil sends a telegram to Lord Henry informing him that Dorian has been injured in a terrible accident.
- D. Dorian sends a telegram to Lord Henry announcing his engagement to Sibyl Vane.

C 15. When Lord Henry and Basil accompany Dorian to the theatre, what happens to make Dorian angry?
- A. They are late arriving from dinner and are not allowed to enter during the show.
- B. Sibyl is so convincing as Juliet that Dorian has become jealous of "Romeo."
- C. Sibyl's performance is terrible. Lord Henry and Basil leave during the show.
- D. That night's performance has been cancelled.

B 16. After he breaks off his relationship with Sibyl, what does Dorian notice about the painting Basil had done of him?
   A. The painting has changed, and on the face of the painting there are tears in the eyes.
   B. The painting has changed, and on the face of the painting there was a touch of cruelty in the mouth.
   C. A black mold is beginning to form around the lower corners of the painting.
   D. Someone has tampered with the painting and marred its appearance.

D 17. What news is in Lord Henry's letter that Dorian does not open?
   A. Basil Hallward is missing.
   B. Lord Henry's wife has asked for a divorce and is leaving him.
   C. The Duchess is so angry with Dorian for standing her up that she vowed to ruin his reputation.
   D. Lord Henry's note says he has learned that Sibyl Vane died in an incident at the theater.

B 18. Who does Basil blame for the changes in Dorian?
   A. Himself
   B. Lord Henry
   C. Sibyl Vane
   D. The Duchess

C 19. Dorian threatens never to speak to Basil again. Why?
   A. Basil blames Dorian for Sibyl's death and wants Dorian to repent his sins.
   B. Basil wants to tell Lord Henry to stay away from Dorian.
   C. Dorian doesn't want Basil to see the painting, so he threatens never to speak to Basil again if Basil looks at it.
   D. Basil threatens to tell Dorian's grandfather about the difficulties Dorian is going through.

C 20. What happens to Dorian Gray?
   A. Dorian is arrested for the murder of Basil Hallward and is hanged.
   B. Dorian is killed by Lord Henry when Henry sees the painting.
   C. Dorian dies while trying to destroy the portrait.
   D. Dorian accidentally falls on the knife that he used to kill Basil.

IV. Vocabulary

P	1.	ENSCONCED	A.	Having an offensive odor; stinking
O	2.	MALADIES	B.	Filthy or dirty; foul
I	3.	UNCOUTH	C.	Area overgrown with ferns and shrubs
G	4.	ENTREAT	D.	Feeling abandoned; forlorn
S	5.	PROTEGE	E.	Fill with water and sink
B	6.	SORDID	F.	Diminished or became tainted
D	7.	DESOLATE	G.	To ask (a person) earnestly; beseech; implore
R	8.	INVARIABLY	H.	Person who promotes or holds religious revivals
L	9.	HANSOM	I.	Awkward, clumsy, or unmannerly
N	10.	IMPASSIVE	J.	Greenhouse, usually attached to a dwelling
K	11.	CENSURE	K.	Criticize or reproach harshly
F	12.	TARNISHED	L.	Two-wheeled covered carriage with the driver's seat above and behind
M	13.	PARODY	M.	Imitate for purposes of ridicule or satire
A	14.	FETID	N.	Without emotion; apathetic; unmoved
J	15.	CONSERVATORY	O.	Undesirable conditions or disorders
T	16.	ABDICATE	P.	Settled securely or snugly
E	17.	FOUNDER	Q.	Strike down, injure, or slay
C	18.	BRACKEN	R.	Without variation or change, in every case
H	19.	REVIVALIST	S.	One whose welfare is promoted by an influential person
Q	20.	SMITE	T.	Renounce or relinquish a throne, right, or power

The Picture of Dorian Gray MULTIPLE CHOICE UNIT TEST 2

I. Matching

____ 1. BASIL   A. Author
____ 2. HENRY   B. Lord Henry's wife
____ 3. DORIAN   C. He had a negative influence on Dorian: Lord ___.
____ 4. FATHER   D. Person who asks Lord Henry how to become young again
____ 5. ERSKINE   E. He claims Lord Henry is extremely dangerous.
____ 6. VICTORIA   F. He leaves the smoking room when Dorian arrives.
____ 7. SYBIL   G. He wants to kill Dorian.
____ 8. JULIET   H. He disposes of Basil's body.
____ 9. ISAACS   I. He painted the portrait of Dorian Gray.
____ 10. DUCHESS   J. Young peasant girl Dorian chooses to leave while she is still pure
____ 11. JAMES   K. Dorian's was killed in a duel.
____ 12. LEAF   L. She commits suicide.
____ 13. BERWICK   M. He shoots the man hiding in the thicket.
____ 14. CAMPBELL   N. He advances Sibyl's family 50 pounds.
____ 15. NARBOROUGH   O. He murders Basil.
____ 16. SINGLETON   P. She thinks living in the country is boring.
____ 17. CLOUSTON   Q. Dorian's housekeeper
____ 18. HETTY   R. Last name of Sibyl and James
____ 19. WILDE   S. Sibyl's theater role
____ 20. VANE   T. He sees Dorian at the opium house.

II. Multiple Choice

1. Why doesn't Basil want to introduce Lord Henry to Dorian Gray?
    A. Basil is afraid for Dorian's safety.
    B. Lord Henry is an evil old man who would ruin Dorian's reputation.
    C. Basil is afraid that Lord Henry will be a negative influence on the young Dorian.
    D. Lord Henry is a known thief, and Basil wants to protect Dorian from involvement.

2. What does Basil implore Dorian to do after seeing the condition of the painting?
    A. Basil begs Dorian to give the painting to museum.
    B. Basil begs Dorian to get on his knees and pray to God for forgiveness of his sins.
    C. Basil begs Dorian to dispose of the painting.
    D. Basil begs Dorian to burn it to send the satyr back to hell where he belongs.

3. What does Dorian Gray do to Basil?
    A. Dorian tells Basil to leave and never return.
    B. Dorian shoves Basil out of the room, and Basil accidentally falls down the stairs and breaks his neck.
    C. Dorian breaks down in tears and prays for Basil's forgiveness.
    D. Dorian viciously stabs Basil in the neck with an artist's knife.

4. What request does Dorian Gray make of Alan Campbell?
    A. Dorian wants Alan to pose as Basil for several days around London so that people will think that Basil is still alive; meanwhile, Dorian will go to Paris, creating an alibi.
    B. Dorian wants Alan to accompany him to Paris and pretend to be Basil Hallward.
    C. Dorian asks Alan Campbell to dispose of Basil's body.
    D. Dorian wants Alan to claim responsibility for Basil's death.

5. Whom does Lady Narbourough accuse of being "extremely wicked"?
    A. Lord Henry
    B. Her husband
    C. Dorian Gray
    D. Basil Hallward

6. Who is the drunken sailor who accused Dorian Gray in the street?
    A. The drunken sailor is James Vane, Sibyl Vane's older brother.
    B. The drunken sailor is Lord Henry's cousin.
    C. The drunken sailor is a former friend of Dorian whose reputation was ruined.
    D. The drunken sailor is Basil's son.

7. What does Dorian Gray blame for raising "such fearful phantoms" that keep him in his house for three days?
    A. He blames Basil Hallward.
    B. He blames his conscience.
    C. He blames Lord Henry's influence.
    D. He blames James Vane.

8. What does Dorian claim is "a terrible reality . . . [that] . . . can be bought, and sold, and bartered away"?
    A. Love
    B. The soul
    C. Faith
    D. Conscience

9. Why does Dorian go to his portrait while thinking of Hetty Merton?
    A. Dorian goes to pack the painting away so he can start over without the painting reminding him of his old ways.
    B. Dorian goes to move the painting to another room in the house so he will never have to see it again.
    C. Dorian believes because he is trying to change the portrait will also change.
    D. Dorain goes to destroy the painting.

10. What does Basil claim that he would have to see before he could believe anything he's heard about Dorian's activities?
    A. Basil claims that he would have to see Dorian's soul.
    B. Basil claims he would have to read Dorian's diary.
    C. Basil claims he would have to speak to Dorian's servants.
    D. Basil claims he would have to see the portrait he painted of Dorian.

11. What sort of fate have many of Dorian's acquaintances met?
    A. Many of his former friends were murdered by Dorian's worst acquaintances.
    B. Most have left the country in disgrace.
    C. Those who were closest to Dorian have lost their respectable reputations in society.
    D. Many have enjoyed basking in Dorian's limelight and have increased their social standing.

12. What does Dorian Gray so desperately wish for that he "would give [his] soul" to have it come true?
    A. Dorian wishes to meet and marry his soul mate.
    B. Dorian wishes that his portrait would age while he remains young and untouched by the ugliness of life.
    C. Dorian wishes that he could travel to America to study the Transcendentalists.
    D. Dorian wishes for enough riches so that he will never have to work.

13. What news is in the telegram that Lord Henry receives from Dorian?
    A. Basil sends a telegram to Lord Henry informing him that Dorian has been injured in a terrible accident.
    B. Dorian sends a telegram to Lord Henry announcing his engagement to Sibyl Vane.
    C. Lord Henry's wife sends him a telegram informing him that she has run away with Dorian.
    D. Basil sends Lord Henry a telegram letting him know that Dorian has agreed to let Basil see the painting.

14. What does it mean to be "good," according to Lord Henry?
    A. To be good is to be in harmony with oneself.
    B. To be good means to work hard for what you have.
    C. To be good is to do one's best to maintain youth and beauty at all costs.
    D. To be good is to be kind and charitable to others.

15. After he breaks off his relationship with Sibyl, what does Dorian notice about the painting Basil had done of him?
    A. The painting has changed, and on the face of the painting there are tears in the eyes.
    B. The painting has changed, and on the face of the painting there was a touch of cruelty in the mouth.
    C. Someone has tampered with the painting and marred its appearance.
    D. A black mold is beginning to form around the lower corners of the painting.

16. What news is in Lord Henry's letter that Dorian does not open?
    A. Lord Henry's wife has asked for a divorce and is leaving him.
    B. Basil Hallward is missing.
    C. The Duchess is so angry with Dorian for standing her up that she vowed to ruin his reputation.
    D. Lord Henry's note says he has learned that Sibyl Vane died in an incident at the theater.

17. Who does Basil blame for the changes in Dorian?
    A. Sibyl Vane
    B. Himself
    C. Lord Henry
    D. The Duchess

18. Why do people tend to disbelieve the rumors about Dorian Gray?
    A. He piously attends Mass daily.
    B. His donations to charity are very generous.
    C. He is a very dedicated worker who never neglects his duties.
    D. His youthful beauty keeps people from believing the worst about him.

19. Which is NOT one of the activities or interests that managed to capture Dorian Gray's attention in his study of the senses?
    A. Catholic ritual
    B. Zoology
    C. Gemstones
    D. Tapestries

20. What happens to Dorian Gray?
    A. Dorian dies while trying to destroy the portrait.
    B. Dorian is arrested for the murder of Basil Hallward and is hanged.
    C. Dorian accidentally falls on the knife that he used to kill Basil.
    D. Dorian is killed by Lord Henry when Henry sees the painting.

III. Composition
1. Why is Lord Henry Wotton also fascinated with Dorian Gray? What is Lord Henry's role in creating the main conflict of the novel? What does this demonstrate about his character?

2. Where is the climax of this novel? Explain your choice.

IV. Vocabulary

____ 1. LANGUIDLY   A. Soft and limp; not firm; flabby

____ 2. PHILANTHROPY   B. Effort or inclination to increase the well-being of humankind

____ 3. APHORISMS   C. Obtained or gotten by care, effort, or the use of special means

____ 4. TAWDRY   D. Gaudy; showy and cheap

____ 5. OMNIBUS   E. Closed four-wheeled carriage with an open driver's seat in the front

____ 6. DEGRADATION   F. Not mixed with impurities; without qualification

____ 7. BROUGHAM   G. State of having little or no money; penniless; poor

____ 8. ELOCUTION   H. Cheerfully optimistic, hopeful, or confident

____ 9. SANGUINE   I. Vehicle carrying many passengers, used for public transport

____ 10. EPIGRAM   J. Destroys completely

____ 11. MISANTHROPE   K. Concise, clever, often paradoxical statement

____ 12. IMPECUNIOSITY   L. Extremly bad reputation

____ 13. FLACCID   M. Tersely phrased statements of truth or opinion; adages

____ 14. PROCURED   N. A decline to a lower condition, quality, or level

____ 15. UNADULTERATED   O. Hater of humankind

____ 16. CORROBORATIVE   P. Person's manner of speaking or reading aloud in public

____ 17. ATONEMENT   Q. Serving to support or to make more certain

____ 18. INFAMY   R. Amends or reparation made for an injury or wrong

____ 19. PRESENTIMENT   S. Feeling of evil to come

____ 20. ANNIHILATES   T. In a manner lacking in spirit or interest; listlessly; indifferently

The Picture of Dorian Gray MULTIPLE CHOICE UNIT TEST 2 Answer Key

I. Matching

I	1.	BASIL	A.	Author
C	2.	HENRY	B.	Lord Henry's wife
O	3.	DORIAN	C.	He had a negative influence on Dorian: Lord ___.
K	4.	FATHER	D.	Person who asks Lord Henry how to become young again
E	5.	ERSKINE	E.	He claims Lord Henry is extremely dangerous.
B	6.	VICTORIA	F.	He leaves the smoking room when Dorian arrives.
L	7.	SYBIL	G.	He wants to kill Dorian.
S	8.	JULIET	H.	He disposes of Basil's body.
N	9.	ISAACS	I.	He painted the portrait of Dorian Gray.
D	10.	DUCHESS	J.	Young peasant girl Dorian chooses to leave while she is still pure
G	11.	JAMES	K.	Dorian's was killed in a duel.
Q	12.	LEAF	L.	She commits suicide.
F	13.	BERWICK	M.	He shoots the man hiding in the thicket.
H	14.	CAMPBELL	N.	He advances Sibyl's family 50 pounds.
P	15.	NARBOROUGH	O.	He murders Basil.
T	16.	SINGLETON	P.	She thinks living in the country is boring.
M	17.	CLOUSTON	Q.	Dorian's housekeeper
J	18.	HETTY	R.	Last name of Sibyl and James
A	19.	WILDE	S.	Sibyl's theater role
R	20.	VANE	T.	He sees Dorian at the opium house.

II. Multiple Choice

C 1. Why doesn't Basil want to introduce Lord Henry to Dorian Gray?
- A. Basil is afraid for Dorian's safety.
- B. Lord Henry is an evil old man who would ruin Dorian's reputation.
- C. Basil is afraid that Lord Henry will be a negative influence on the young Dorian.
- D. Lord Henry is a known thief, and Basil wants to protect Dorian from involvement.

B 2. What does Basil implore Dorian to do after seeing the condition of the painting?
- A. Basil begs Dorian to give the painting to museum.
- B. Basil begs Dorian to get on his knees and pray to God for forgiveness of his sins.
- C. Basil begs Dorian to dispose of the painting.
- D. Basil begs Dorian to burn it to send the satyr back to hell where he belongs.

D 3. What does Dorian Gray do to Basil?
- A. Dorian tells Basil to leave and never return.
- B. Dorian shoves Basil out of the room, and Basil accidentally falls down the stairs and breaks his neck.
- C. Dorian breaks down in tears and prays for Basil's forgiveness.
- D. Dorian viciously stabs Basil in the neck with an artist's knife.

C 4. What request does Dorian Gray make of Alan Campbell?
- A. Dorian wants Alan to pose as Basil for several days around London so that people will think that Basil is still alive; meanwhile, Dorian will go to Paris, creating an alibi.
- B. Dorian wants Alan to accompany him to Paris and pretend to be Basil Hallward.
- C. Dorian asks Alan Campbell to dispose of Basil's body.
- D. Dorian wants Alan to claim responsibility for Basil's death.

A 5. Whom does Lady Narbourough accuse of being "extremely wicked"?
- A. Lord Henry
- B. Her husband
- C. Dorian Gray
- D. Basil Hallward

A 6. Who is the drunken sailor who accused Dorian Gray in the street?
   A. The drunken sailor is James Vane, Sibyl Vane's older brother.
   B. The drunken sailor is Lord Henry's cousin.
   C. The drunken sailor is a former friend of Dorian whose reputation was ruined.
   D. The drunken sailor is Basil's son.

B 7. What does Dorian Gray blame for raising "such fearful phantoms" that keep him in his house for three days?
   A. He blames Basil Hallward.
   B. He blames his conscience.
   C. He blames Lord Henry's influence.
   D. He blames James Vane.

B 8. What does Dorian claim is "a terrible reality . . . [that] . . . can be bought, and sold, and bartered away"?
   A. Love
   B. The soul
   C. Faith
   D. Conscience

C 9. Why does Dorian go to his portrait while thinking of Hetty Merton?
   A. Dorian goes to pack the painting away so he can start over without the painting reminding him of his old ways.
   B. Dorian goes to move the painting to another room in the house so he will never have to see it again.
   C. Dorian believes because he is trying to change the portrait will also change.
   D. Dorain goes to destroy the painting.

A 10. What does Basil claim that he would have to see before he could believe anything he's heard about Dorian's activities?
   A. Basil claims that he would have to see Dorian's soul.
   B. Basil claims he would have to read Dorian's diary.
   C. Basil claims he would have to speak to Dorian's servants.
   D. Basil claims he would have to see the portrait he painted of Dorian.

C 11. What sort of fate have many of Dorian's acquaintances met?
- A. Many of his former friends were murdered by Dorian's worst acquaintances.
- B. Most have left the country in disgrace.
- C. Those who were closest to Dorian have lost their respectable reputations in society.
- D. Many have enjoyed basking in Dorian's limelight and have increased their social standing.

B 12. What does Dorian Gray so desperately wish for that he "would give [his] soul" to have it come true?
- A. Dorian wishes to meet and marry his soul mate.
- B. Dorian wishes that his portrait would age while he remains young and untouched by the ugliness of life.
- C. Dorian wishes that he could travel to America to study the Transcendentalists.
- D. Dorian wishes for enough riches so that he will never have to work.

B 13. What news is in the telegram that Lord Henry receives from Dorian?
- A. Basil sends a telegram to Lord Henry informing him that Dorian has been injured in a terrible accident.
- B. Dorian sends a telegram to Lord Henry announcing his engagement to Sibyl Vane.
- C. Lord Henry's wife sends him a telegram informing him that she has run away with Dorian.
- D. Basil sends Lord Henry a telegram letting him know that Dorian has agreed to let Basil see the painting.

A 14. What does it mean to be "good," according to Lord Henry?
- A. To be good is to be in harmony with oneself.
- B. To be good means to work hard for what you have.
- C. To be good is to do one's best to maintain youth and beauty at all costs.
- D. To be good is to be kind and charitable to others.

B 15. After he breaks off his relationship with Sibyl, what does Dorian notice about the painting Basil had done of him?
- A. The painting has changed, and on the face of the painting there are tears in the eyes.
- B. The painting has changed, and on the face of the painting there was a touch of cruelty in the mouth.
- C. Someone has tampered with the painting and marred its appearance.
- D. A black mold is beginning to form around the lower corners of the painting.

D 16. What news is in Lord Henry's letter that Dorian does not open?
- A. Lord Henry's wife has asked for a divorce and is leaving him.
- B. Basil Hallward is missing.
- C. The Duchess is so angry with Dorian for standing her up that she vowed to ruin his reputation.
- D. Lord Henry's note says he has learned that Sibyl Vane died in an incident at the theater.

C 17. Who does Basil blame for the changes in Dorian?
- A. Sibyl Vane
- B. Himself
- C. Lord Henry
- D. The Duchess

D 18. Why do people tend to disbelieve the rumors about Dorian Gray?
- A. He piously attends Mass daily.
- B. His donations to charity are very generous.
- C. He is a very dedicated worker who never neglects his duties.
- D. His youthful beauty keeps people from believing the worst about him.

B 19. Which is NOT one of the activities or interests that managed to capture Dorian Gray's attention in his study of the senses?
- A. Catholic ritual
- B. Zoology
- C. Gemstones
- D. Tapestries

A 20. What happens to Dorian Gray?
- A. Dorian dies while trying to destroy the portrait.
- B. Dorian is arrested for the murder of Basil Hallward and is hanged.
- C. Dorian accidentally falls on the knife that he used to kill Basil.
- D. Dorian is killed by Lord Henry when Henry sees the painting.

IV. Vocabulary

T	1. LANGUIDLY	A.	Soft and limp; not firm; flabby
B	2. PHILANTHROPY	B.	Effort or inclination to increase the well-being of humankind
M	3. APHORISMS	C.	Obtained or gotten by care, effort, or the use of special means
D	4. TAWDRY	D.	Gaudy; showy and cheap
I	5. OMNIBUS	E.	Closed four-wheeled carriage with an open driver's seat in the front
N	6. DEGRADATION	F.	Not mixed with impurities; without qualification
E	7. BROUGHAM	G.	State of having little or no money; penniless; poor
P	8. ELOCUTION	H.	Cheerfully optimistic, hopeful, or confident
H	9. SANGUINE	I.	Vehicle carrying many passengers, used for public transport
K	10. EPIGRAM	J.	Destroys completely
O	11. MISANTHROPE	K.	Concise, clever, often paradoxical statement
G	12. IMPECUNIOSITY	L.	Extremly bad reputation
A	13. FLACCID	M.	Tersely phrased statements of truth or opinion; adages
C	14. PROCURED	N.	A decline to a lower condition, quality, or level
F	15. UNADULTERATED	O.	Hater of humankind
Q	16. CORROBORATIVE	P.	Person's manner of speaking or reading aloud in public
R	17. ATONEMENT	Q.	Serving to support or to make more certain
L	18. INFAMY	R.	Amends or reparation made for an injury or wrong
S	19. PRESENTIMENT	S.	Feeling of evil to come
J	20. ANNIHILATES	T.	In a manner lacking in spirit or interest; listlessly; indifferently

UNIT RESOURCE MATERIALS

BULLETIN BOARD IDEAS *The Picture of Dorian Gray*

1. Save a corner of the board for the best of students' *The Picture of Dorian Gray* writing assignments.
2. Take one of the word search puzzles from the extra activities packet and with a marker copy it over it a large size on the bulletin board. Write the clue words to find to one side. Invite students prior to and after class to find the worlds and circle them on the bulletin board.
3. Write several of the most significant quotations from the book onto the board on brightly colored paper.
4. Make a bulletin board listing the vocabulary words for this unit. As you complete sections of the novel and discuss the vocabulary for each section, write the definitions on the bulletin board. (If your board is one students face frequently, it will help them learn the words.)
5. Make a large portrait of Dorian Gray for the bulletin board. As the novel progresses have students make changes to the picture reflecting events in the story.
6. Have students create a bulletin board devoted to the works of Carl Jung, particularly the "shadow." Students could draw pictures of their own shadow selves if they wish.
7. Create a bulletin board devoted to the idea of the "Doppelganger." Have students decorate with as many examples from literature or movies as they can.
8. Have students create a bulletin board devoted to the Gothic literature genre, being sure to identify elements of a Gothic novel.
9. Have students create a large scandal sheet on a bulletin board, displaying their articles they've written about the characters in the novel. Don't forget a catchy title for the scandal sheet and pictures.
10. Display the characterization posters that students made.
11. It may be argued that Dorian's downfall can be partially attributed to the negative influence of Lord Henry Wotton's praises regarding Dorian's beauty and youth. These words might be seen as seeds planted in Dorian's mind that sprouted and grew into the weeds that choked out his soul. Create a progressive bulletin board exploring this concept, being sure to label incidents in the novel to each step of the growing process.

MORE ACTIVITIES *The Picture of Dorian Gray*

1. Have students work together to make a timeline chronology of the events in the story. Take a large piece of construction paper and on one wall (or however you can physically arrange it in your room) and make the events of the story along it. Students may want to add drawings or cur-out pictures to represent the events (as well as a written statement).

2. Have students design a book cover (front and back inside flaps) for *The Picture of Dorian Gray*.

3. Have students desgin a bulletin board (ready to be put up; not just sketched) for *The Picture of Dorian Gray*.

4. Have students group the books together to show the larger structure of the novel. Have them explain why they choose the divisions they made.

5. Have students choose one chapter from the novel (with sufficient dialogue) to rewrite as a play. In conjunction with this assignment, have students write a comparison explaining the difficulties they encountered in changing from one written form to another.

6. Have students create journals of at least five entries for various characters in the novel. Be sure to use an appropriate voice for the character as well as incorporate as many vocabulary words as possible.

7. Watch a film version of *The Picture of Dorian Gray* and have students relate the film to the novel. How true was the screenwriter to Oscar Wilde's original?

8. Obtain a CD of *Dorian Gray: The Musical*. Make copies of lyrics to some of the songs and have students determine how true the lyrics are to the character who sings them. Was the lyricist true to Oscar Wilde's characterization?

9. Eleanor Roosevelt once said, "Beautiful young people are an accident of nature. Beautiful old people are works of art." What does she mean by her words? Apply the main idea of Roosevelt's quotation to *The Picture of Dorian Gray*.

10. Watch the film *The League of Extraordinary Gentlemen*. How does the screenwriter's portrayal of Dorian Gray's character compare to Oscar Wilde's characterization?

UNIT WORD LIST *The Picture of Dorian Gray*

No.	Word	Clue/Definition
1.	BASIL	He painted the portrait of Dorian Gray.
2.	BEAUTY	Lord Henry tells Dorian the secret of life is the search for this.
3.	BERWICK	He leaves the smoking room when Dorian arrives.
4.	BOOK	It has a huge influence on Dorian's behavior.
5.	CAMPBELL	He disposes of Basil's body.
6.	CLOUSTON	He shoots the man hiding in the thicket.
7.	CORONER	Rules Sibyl's death a accident
8.	CRUELTY	The portrait showed this in the mouth.
9.	DORIAN	He murders Basil.
10.	DUCHESS	Person who asks Lord Henry how to become young again
11.	ERSKINE	He claims Lord Henry is extremely dangerous.
12.	FATHER	Dorian's was killed in a duel.
13.	GOOD	According to Lord Henry, to be this is to be in harmony with oneself.
14.	HARE	Dorian begs Sir Geoffrey not to shoot this.
15.	HENRY	He had a negative influence on Dorian: Lord ___.
16.	HETTY	Young peasant girl Dorian chooses to leave while she is still pure
17.	ISAACS	He advances Sibyl's family 50 pounds.
18.	JAMES	He wants to kill Dorian.
19.	JULIET	Sibyl's theater role
20.	LEAF	Dorian's housekeeper
21.	NARBOROUGH	She thinks living in the country is boring.
22.	OPERA	Dorian goes there after he learns of Sibyl's death.
23.	PARIS	Basil wants to exhibit Dorian's portrait there.
24.	PORTRAIT	Visual diary of Dorian's soul
25.	PRINCE	Sibyl knows Dorian by this 'Charming' name.
26.	REALITY	It spoiled Sibyl's acting.
27.	RINGS	Dorian's servants can only identify his body by these.
28.	SATYR	Basil sees this in his portrait of Dorian.
29.	SHAME	Dorian chooses to allow the painting to bear the burden of his ___.
30.	SINGLETON	He sees Dorian at the opium house.
31.	SINS	Dorian believes that forgivenesss for these is impossible.
32.	SOUL	Dorian claims this can be bought, sold, and bartered away.
33.	SPHINXES	Lord Henry describes women as these without secrets.
34.	SYBIL	She commits suicide.
35.	TELEGRAM	Dorian sends one to Lord Henry announcing his engagement.
36.	TEMPTATION	According to Lord Henry, the only way to get rid of this is to yeild to it.
37.	UGLY	Lord Henry says it is better to be good than this.

No.	Word	Clue/Definition
38.	UNSELFISH	Lord Henry says these people are colorless and lack individuality.
39.	VANE	Last name of Sibyl and James
40.	VICTORIA	Lord Henry's wife
41.	WAINSCOTING	Dorian hides Basil's belongings behind this.
42.	WILDE	Author
43.	YOUTH	The secret of this is to repeat the follies of it.

WORD SEARCH - The Picture of Dorian Gray

```
C Q B U N S E L F I S H J A M E S Q R W
L A R Q G K X F X Z S D U H I N S M E R
O N M N R L P T C D L T L F S A E M A H
U E D P P L Y K V D S I I P A R H V L Z
S C T S B E R W I C K A E L A B C D I Z
T N R N T E K J T M W R T R C O U R T W
O I B U L V L Y E Z A T P Y S R D V Y T
N R J Q E D B L L F I R M S R O V X R D
H P L R P L Q B E L N O H F Y U S W S V
J E M E E W T Y G Q S P S M N G W E Z P
K Z T M A F R Y R K C V X R N H X N H R
Z K A T C F W P A W O N K I V N S P L N
F H L F Y T Q C M W T K R G I L J C W F
S F T G J L Y J K S I G Q H K Q C J V B
J H E D B P D F G I N Q P F R N B J V M
C H M W E C P N V N G S M T W L N S I K
D D P Y R F J M H G H D Q W G L B G C W
O V T Q S A C G R L J D H S N F E B T R
R P A K K T B O Z E H W E L G A L O C
I X T X I H B S R T S R I T N S U U R D
A Y I D N E I O S O I L L Q I R T O I H
N S O P E R A V O N N J D L I B Y S A M
D O N U A P V A S K S E E K L Y P R W M
G T P P T G W N V N B D R H C X E J V R
X Y N D K H K E Y M V Z N X D N X Q D G
```

BASIL	DUCHESS	JULIET	SATYR	UGLY
BEAUTY	ERSKINE	LEAF	SHAME	UNSELFISH
BERWICK	FATHER	NARBOROUGH	SINGLETON	VANE
BOOK	GOOD	OPERA	SINS	VICTORIA
CAMPBELL	HARE	PARIS	SOUL	WAINSCOTING
CLOUSTON	HENRY	PORTRAIT	SPHINXES	WILDE
CORONER	HETTY	PRINCE	SYBIL	YOUTH
CRUELTY	ISAACS	REALITY	TELEGRAM	
DORIAN	JAMES	RINGS	TEMPTATION	

WORD SEARCH ANSWER KEY - The Picture of Dorian Gray

BASIL	DUCHESS	JULIET	SATYR	UGLY
BEAUTY	ERSKINE	LEAF	SHAME	UNSELFISH
BERWICK	FATHER	NARBOROUGH	SINGLETON	VANE
BOOK	GOOD	OPERA	SINS	VICTORIA
CAMPBELL	HARE	PARIS	SOUL	WAINSCOTING
CLOUSTON	HENRY	PORTRAIT	SPHINXES	WILDE
CORONER	HETTY	PRINCE	SYBIL	YOUTH
CRUELTY	ISAACS	REALITY	TELEGRAM	
DORIAN	JAMES	RINGS	TEMPTATION	

CROSSWORD - The Picture of Dorian Gray

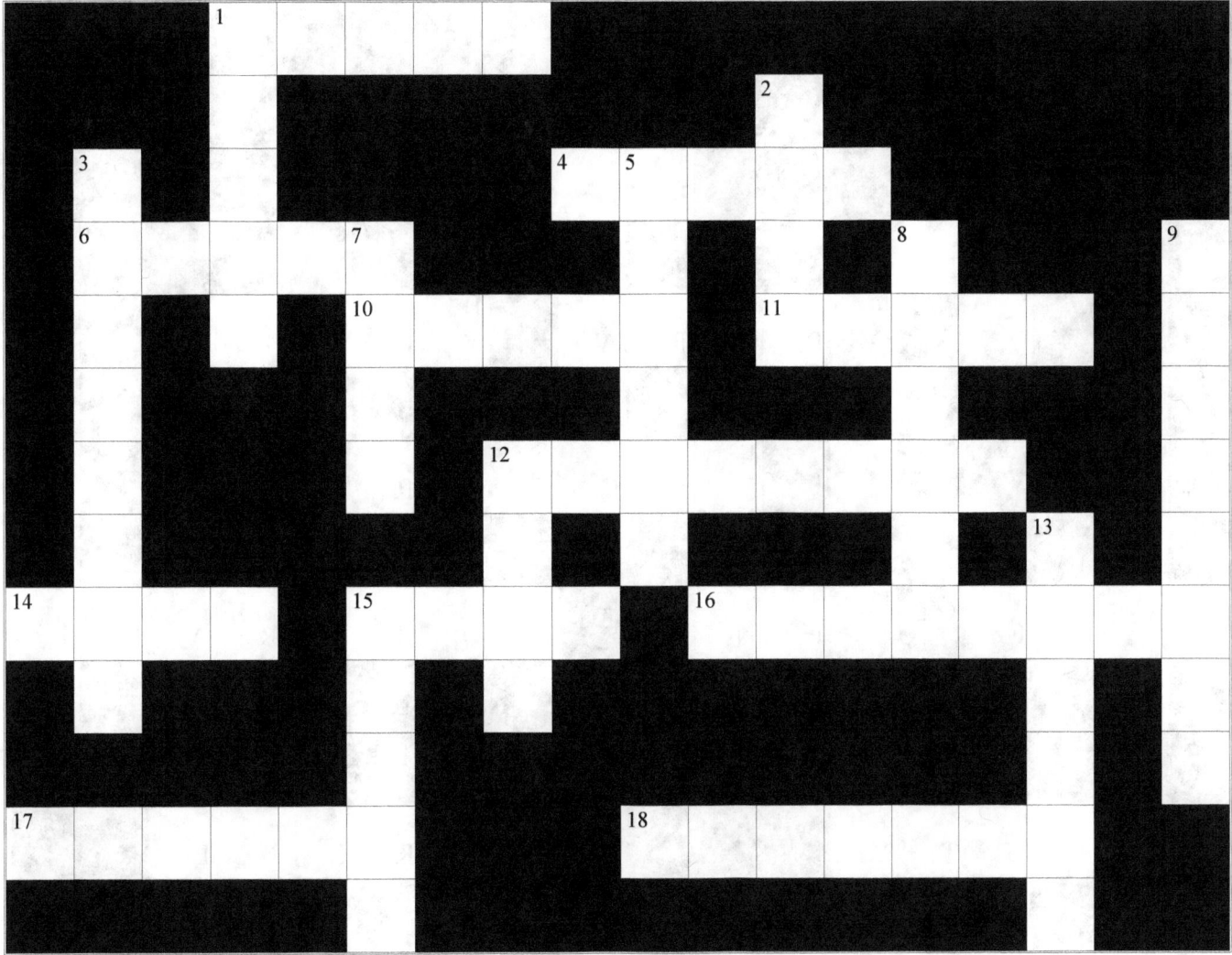

Across

1. Young peasant girl Dorian chooses to leave while she is still pure
4. Dorian's servants can only identify his body by these.
6. Basil wants to exhibit Dorian's portrait there.
10. Dorian goes there after he learns of Sibyl's death.
11. The secret of this is to repeat the follies of it.
12. Lord Henry's wife
14. Dorian's housekeeper
15. Dorian believes that forgiveness for these is impossible.
16. Visual diary of Dorian's soul
17. Lord Henry tells Dorian the secret of life is the search for this.
18. He claims Lord Henry is extremely dangerous.

Down

1. He has a negative influence on Dorian: Lord ___.
2. Lord Henry says it is better to be good than this.
3. Lord Henry describes women as these without secrets.
5. He advances Sibyl's family 50 pounds.
7. Dorian claims this can be bought, sold, and bartered away.
8. Sibyl's theater role
9. He shoots the man hiding in the thicket.
12. Last name of Sibyl and James
13. Dorian's was killed in a duel.
15. Basil sees this in his portrait of Dorian.

CROSSWORD ANSWER KEY - The Picture of Dorian Gray

			1 H	E	T	T	Y										
			E								2 U						
	3 S		N					4 R	5 I	N	G	S					
	6 P	A	R	I	7 S				S		L		8 J				9 C
	H		Y		10 O	P	E	R	A		11 Y	O	U	T	H		L
	I				U				A				L				O
	N				L		12 V	I	C	T	O	R	I	A			U
	X						A		S				E		13 F		S
14 L	E	A	F		15 S	I	N	S		16 P	O	R	T	R	A	I	T
	S				A		E								T		O
					T										H		N
17 B	E	A	U	T	Y				18 E	R	S	K	I	N	E		
					R										R		

Across

1. Young peasant girl Dorian chooses to leave while she is still pure
4. Dorian's servants can only identify his body by these.
6. Basil wants to exhibit Dorian's portrait there.
10. Dorian goes there after he learns of Sibyl's death.
11. The secret of this is to repeat the follies of it.
12. Lord Henry's wife
14. Dorian's housekeeper
15. Dorian believes that forgiveness for these is impossible.
16. Visual diary of Dorian's soul
17. Lord Henry tells Dorian the secret of life is the search for this.
18. He claims Lord Henry is extremely dangerous.

Down

1. He has a negative influence on Dorian: Lord ___.
2. Lord Henry says it is better to be good than this.
3. Lord Henry describes women as these without secrets.
5. He advances Sibyl's family 50 pounds.
7. Dorian claims this can be bought, sold, and bartered away.
8. Sibyl's theater role
9. He shoots the man hiding in the thicket.
12. Last name of Sibyl and James
13. Dorian's was killed in a duel.
15. Basil sees this in his portrait of Dorian.

MATCHING 1 *The Picture of Dorian Gray*

____ 1. VANE   A. She commits suicide.

____ 2. ISAACS   B. Author

____ 3. JULIET   C. Person who asks Lord Henry how to become young again

____ 4. SYBIL   D. He claims Lord Henry is extremely dangerous.

____ 5. VICTORIA   E. He sees Dorian at the opium house.

____ 6. ERSKINE   F. He had a negative influence on Dorian: Lord ___.

____ 7. FATHER   G. He murders Basil.

____ 8. DORIAN   H. Last name of Sibyl and James

____ 9. HENRY   I. She thinks living in the country is boring.

____ 10. DUCHESS   J. He wants to kill Dorian.

____ 11. JAMES   K. He painted the portrait of Dorian Gray.

____ 12. WILDE   L. He disposes of Basil's body.

____ 13. HETTY   M. Young peasant girl Dorian chooses to leave while she is still pure

____ 14. CLOUSTON   N. Sibyl's theater role

____ 15. SINGLETON   O. Lord Henry's wife

____ 16. NARBOROUGH   P. He leaves the smoking room when Dorian arrives.

____ 17. CAMPBELL   Q. He shoots the man hiding in the thicket.

____ 18. BERWICK   R. Rules Sibyl's death a accident

____ 19. CORONER   S. Dorian's was killed in a duel.

____ 20. BASIL   T. He advances Sibyl's family 50 pounds.

MATCHING 1 ANSWER KEY *The Picture of Dorian Gray*

H	1.	VANE	A.	She commits suicide.
T	2.	ISAACS	B.	Author
N	3.	JULIET	C.	Person who asks Lord Henry how to become young again
A	4.	SYBIL	D.	He claims Lord Henry is extremely dangerous.
O	5.	VICTORIA	E.	He sees Dorian at the opium house.
D	6.	ERSKINE	F.	He had a negative influence on Dorian: Lord ___.
S	7.	FATHER	G.	He murders Basil.
G	8.	DORIAN	H.	Last name of Sibyl and James
F	9.	HENRY	I.	She thinks living in the country is boring.
C	10.	DUCHESS	J.	He wants to kill Dorian.
J	11.	JAMES	K.	He painted the portrait of Dorian Gray.
B	12.	WILDE	L.	He disposes of Basil's body.
M	13.	HETTY	M.	Young peasant girl Dorian chooses to leave while she is still pure
Q	14.	CLOUSTON	N.	Sibyl's theater role
E	15.	SINGLETON	O.	Lord Henry's wife
I	16.	NARBOROUGH	P.	He leaves the smoking room when Dorian arrives.
L	17.	CAMPBELL	Q.	He shoots the man hiding in the thicket.
P	18.	BERWICK	R.	Rules Sibyl's death a accident
R	19.	CORONER	S.	Dorian's was killed in a duel.
K	20.	BASIL	T.	He advances Sibyl's family 50 pounds.

MATCHING 2 *The Picture of Dorian Gray*

____ 1. SPHINXES   A. Author

____ 2. SYBIL   B. According to Lord Henry, to be this is to be in harmony with oneself.

____ 3. YOUTH   C. It spoiled Sibyl's acting.

____ 4. FATHER   D. He painted the portrait of Dorian Gray.

____ 5. TEMPTATION   E. Dorian's was killed in a duel.

____ 6. PORTRAIT   F. He wants to kill Dorian.

____ 7. SOUL   G. She commits suicide.

____ 8. DORIAN   H. Lord Henry says these people are colorless and lack individuality.

____ 9. HENRY   I. Lord Henry describes women as these without secrets.

____ 10. BEAUTY   J. He had a negative influence on Dorian: Lord ___.

____ 11. TELEGRAM   K. Lord Henry tells Dorian the secret of life is the search for this.

____ 12. REALITY   L. Dorian's housekeeper

____ 13. UNSELFISH   M. He murders Basil.

____ 14. WILDE   N. Dorian sends one to Lord Henry announcing his engagement.

____ 15. RINGS   O. The secret of this is to repeat the follies of it.

____ 16. WAINSCOTING   P. Visual diary of Dorian's soul

____ 17. LEAF   Q. According to Lord Henry, the only way to get rid of this is to yeild to it.

____ 18. JAMES   R. Dorian's servants can only identify his body by these.

____ 19. GOOD   S. Dorian claims this can be bought, sold, and bartered away.

____ 20. BASIL   T. Dorian hides Basil's belongings behind this.

MATCHING 2 ANSWER KEY *The Picture of Dorian Gray*

I	1.	SPHINXES	A.	Author
G	2.	SYBIL	B.	According to Lord Henry, to be this is to be in harmony with oneself.
O	3.	YOUTH	C.	It spoiled Sibyl's acting.
E	4.	FATHER	D.	He painted the portrait of Dorian Gray.
Q	5.	TEMPTATION	E.	Dorian's was killed in a duel.
P	6.	PORTRAIT	F.	He wants to kill Dorian.
S	7.	SOUL	G.	She commits suicide.
M	8.	DORIAN	H.	Lord Henry says these people are colorless and lack individuality.
J	9.	HENRY	I.	Lord Henry describes women as these without secrets.
K	10.	BEAUTY	J.	He had a negative influence on Dorian: Lord ___.
N	11.	TELEGRAM	K.	Lord Henry tells Dorian the secret of life is the search for this.
C	12.	REALITY	L.	Dorian's housekeeper
H	13.	UNSELFISH	M.	He murders Basil.
A	14.	WILDE	N.	Dorian sends one to Lord Henry announcing his engagement.
R	15.	RINGS	O.	The secret of this is to repeat the follies of it.
T	16.	WAINSCOTING	P.	Visual diary of Dorian's soul
L	17.	LEAF	Q.	According to Lord Henry, the only way to get rid of this is to yeild to it.
F	18.	JAMES	R.	Dorian's servants can only identify his body by these.
B	19.	GOOD	S.	Dorian claims this can be bought, sold, and bartered away.
D	20.	BASIL	T.	Dorian hides Basil's belongings behind this.

JUGGLE LETTER 1 *The Picture of Dorian Gray*

_____ = 1. SEMAH
Dorian chooses to allow the painting to bear the burden of his ___.

_____ = 2. IAORDN
He murders Basil.

_____ = 3. MINOTATPET
According to Lord Henry, the only way to get rid of this is to yeild to it.

_____ = 4. HTAEFR
Dorian's was killed in a duel.

_____ = 5. KIESNER
He claims Lord Henry is extremely dangerous.

_____ = 6. LJUTIE
Sibyl's theater role

_____ = 7. AISSAC
He advances Sibyl's family 50 pounds.

_____ = 8. ESHCUSD
Person who asks Lord Henry how to become young again

_____ = 9. ROCERON
Rules Sibyl's death a accident

_____ = 10. ASCGNNWTIIO
Dorian hides Basil's belongings behind this.

_____ = 11. MECPLBAL
He disposes of Basil's body.

_____ = 12. HUOAGOBNRR
She thinks living in the country is boring.

_____ = 13. SNNOGELIT
He sees Dorian at the opium house.

_____ = 14. EDILW
Author

_____ = 15. BASIL
He painted the portrait of Dorian Gray.

JUGGLE LETTER 1 ANSWER KEY *The Picture of Dorian Gray*

SHAME	= 1.	SEMAH
		Dorian chooses to allow the painting to bear the burden of his ___.
DORIAN	= 2.	IAORDN
		He murders Basil.
TEMPTATION	= 3.	MINOTATPET
		According to Lord Henry, the only way to get rid of this is to yeild to it.
FATHER	= 4.	HTAEFR
		Dorian's was killed in a duel.
ERSKINE	= 5.	KIESNER
		He claims Lord Henry is extremely dangerous.
JULIET	= 6.	LJUTIE
		Sibyl's theater role
ISAACS	= 7.	AISSAC
		He advances Sibyl's family 50 pounds.
DUCHESS	= 8.	ESHCUSD
		Person who asks Lord Henry how to become young again
CORONER	= 9.	ROCERON
		Rules Sibyl's death a accident
WAINSCOTING	= 10.	ASCGNNWTIIO
		Dorian hides Basil's belongings behind this.
CAMPBELL	= 11.	MECPLBAL
		He disposes of Basil's body.
NARBOROUGH	= 12.	HUOAGOBNRR
		She thinks living in the country is boring.
SINGLETON	= 13.	SNNOGELIT
		He sees Dorian at the opium house.
WILDE	= 14.	EDILW
		Author
BASIL	= 15.	BASIL
		He painted the portrait of Dorian Gray.

JUGGLE LETTER 2 *The Picture of Dorian Gray*

_____ = 1. REUTYLC
The portrait showed this in the mouth.

_____ = 2. OLSU
Dorian claims this can be bought, sold, and bartered away.

_____ = 3. TPIRTRAO
Visual diary of Dorian's soul

_____ = 4. OHYUT
The secret of this is to repeat the follies of it.

_____ = 5. ORTCVIIA
Lord Henry's wife

_____ = 6. LSYIB
She commits suicide.

_____ = 7. GREETALM
Dorian sends one to Lord Henry announcing his engagement.

_____ = 8. JASME
He wants to kill Dorian.

_____ = 9. PRAEO
Dorian goes there after he learns of Sibyl's death.

_____ = 10. IICASNWTGON
Dorian hides Basil's belongings behind this.

_____ = 11. LLBPCEMA
He disposes of Basil's body.

_____ = 12. LTNSOCUO
He shoots the man hiding in the thicket.

_____ = 13. YEHTT
Young peasant girl Dorian chooses to leave while she is still pure

_____ = 14. IECNPR
Sibyl knows Dorian by this 'Charming' name.

_____ = 15. REYHN
He had a negative influence on Dorian: Lord ___.

JUGGLE LETTER 2 ANSWER KEY *The Picture of Dorian Gray*

CRUELTY	= 1.	REUTYLC
		The portrait showed this in the mouth.
SOUL	= 2.	OLSU
		Dorian claims this can be bought, sold, and bartered away.
PORTRAIT	= 3.	TPIRTRAO
		Visual diary of Dorian's soul
YOUTH	= 4.	OHYUT
		The secret of this is to repeat the follies of it.
VICTORIA	= 5.	ORTCVIIA
		Lord Henry's wife
SYBIL	= 6.	LSYIB
		She commits suicide.
TELEGRAM	= 7.	GREETALM
		Dorian sends one to Lord Henry announcing his engagement.
JAMES	= 8.	JASME
		He wants to kill Dorian.
OPERA	= 9.	PRAEO
		Dorian goes there after he learns of Sibyl's death.
WAINSCOTING	= 10.	IICASNWTGON
		Dorian hides Basil's belongings behind this.
CAMPBELL	= 11.	LLBPCEMA
		He disposes of Basil's body.
CLOUSTON	= 12.	LTNSOCUO
		He shoots the man hiding in the thicket.
HETTY	= 13.	YEHTT
		Young peasant girl Dorian chooses to leave while she is still pure
PRINCE	= 14.	IECNPR
		Sibyl knows Dorian by this 'Charming' name.
HENRY	= 15.	REYHN
		He had a negative influence on Dorian: Lord ___.

VOCABULARY RESOURCE MATERIALS

The Picture of Dorian Gray Vocabulary

No.	Word	Clue/Definition
1.	ABDICATE	Renounce or relinquish a throne, right, or power
2.	AFFINITY	Natural liking for or attraction to a person, thing, idea, etc.
3.	ANNIHILATES	Destroys completely
4.	ANODYNE	Anything that relieves distress or pain
5.	APHORISMS	Tersely phrased statements of truth or opinion; adages
6.	ASPHODEL	Various plants of the lily family
7.	ATONEMENT	Amends or reparation made for an injury or wrong
8.	BALUSTRADE	Railing at the side of a staircase or balcony
9.	BEATERS	People who rouse or drive game from cover
10.	BRACKEN	Area overgrown with ferns and shrubs
11.	BROUGHAM	Closed four-wheeled carriage with an open driver's seat in the front
12.	CAPRICE	An inclination to change one's mind impulsively
13.	CENSURE	Criticize or reproach harshly
14.	CONJECTURES	Judgments based on inconclusive or incomplete evidence
15.	CONSERVATORY	Greenhouse, usually attached to a dwelling
16.	CORROBORATIVE	Serving to support or to make more certain
17.	CRUCIBLE	Severe, searching test or trial
18.	DEBAUCHERY	Excessive indulgence in sensual pleasures
19.	DEGRADATION	A decline to a lower condition, quality, or level
20.	DESOLATE	Feeling abandoned; forlorn
21.	DISDAIN	Feeling of contempt for anything regarded as unworthy
22.	DISENGAGED	Freed from an engagement, pledge, or obligation
23.	DOWAGERS	Widows who hold property derived from deceased husbands
24.	ELOCUTION	Person's manner of speaking or reading aloud in public
25.	ENNUI	Feeling of utter weariness and discontent resulting from satiety or lack of interest; boredom
26.	ENSCONCED	Settled securely or snugly
27.	ENTHRALL	Captivate or charm
28.	ENTREAT	To ask (a person) earnestly; beseech; implore
29.	EPIGRAM	Concise, clever, often paradoxical statement
30.	ESPIAL	Act of watching, especially in secret
31.	EXPOUND	Set forth or state in detail
32.	FACILE	Easily done, performed, or used
33.	FETID	Having an offensive odor; stinking
34.	FIASCO	Complete and humiliting failure
35.	FLACCID	Soft and limp; not firm; flabby
36.	FOLLIES	Foolishness
37.	FOUNDER	Fill with water and sink
38.	GONDOLA	Long narrow flat-bottomed boat propelled by sculling

No.	Word	Clue/Definition
39.	GUFFAWED	Laughed heartily and boisterously
40.	HAGGARD	Having a gaunt, wasted, or exhausted appearance, as from prolonged suffering, exertion, or anxiety
41.	HANSOM	Two-wheeled covered carriage with the driver's seat above and behind
42.	HEDONISM	Devotion to pleasure as a way of life
43.	IDOLATROUS	Having excessive or blind adoration, reverence, or devotion
44.	IDYLL	Simple descriptive or narrative piece in verse or prose
45.	IMPASSIVE	Without emotion; apathetic; unmoved
46.	IMPECUNIOSITY	State of having little or no money; penniless; poor
47.	INCARNATION	Assumption of human form or nature
48.	INCORRIGIBLE	Difficult or impossible to control or manage
49.	INDUCE	To bring about, produce, or cause
50.	INFAMY	Extremly bad reputation
51.	INSOLENCES	Contemptuously rude or impertinent behavior or speech
52.	INTERMINABLE	Seeming to be without an end; endless
53.	INVARIABLY	Without variation or change, in every case
54.	IRRETRIEVABLE	Unable to be recovered or regained
55.	LANGUIDLY	In a manner lacking in spirit or interest; listlessly; indifferently
56.	LIVERIES	Uniforms worn by servants
57.	LUCRATIVE	Producing wealth; profitable
58.	LURID	Gruesome; horrible; revolting
59.	MALADIES	Undesirable conditions or disorders
60.	MEDIOCRITY	State of being ordinary; not outstanding
61.	MISANTHROPE	Hater of humankind
62.	MYRIAD	A very great number of persons or things
63.	OMNIBUS	Vehicle carrying many passengers, used for public transport
64.	ORPHREYS	Ornamental bands or borders, esp. on ecclesiastical vestments
65.	PANEGYRIC	Formal or elaborate praise
66.	PARASOLS	Light, usually small umbrellas carried as protection from the sun
67.	PARODY	Imitate for purposes of ridicule or satire
68.	PATHOS	Feeling of sympathy or pity
69.	PETULANT	Unreasonably irritable or ill-tempered
70.	PHILANTHROPY	Effort or inclination to increase the well-being of humankind
71.	POMPOUS	Characterized by excessive self-esteem or exaggerated dignity
72.	PORTICO	Structure consisting of a roof supported by columns or piers, usually attached to a building as a porch
73.	PRATE	Talk excessively and pointlessly; babble
74.	PRECIPICE	Cliff with a vertical or overhanging face
75.	PRESENTIMENT	Feeling of evil to come

No.	Word	Clue/Definition
76.	PRIG	Self-righteous person who demands pointless conformity
77.	PROCURED	Obtained or gotten by care, effort, or the use of special means
78.	PROFLIGACY	Reckless extravagance
79.	PROTEGE	One whose welfare is promoted by an influential person
80.	PRUDENCE	Caution with regard to practical matters; discretion
81.	QUAY	Landing place constructed along the edge of a body of water
82.	REJOINDER	Answer to a reply; response
83.	REVIVALIST	Person who promotes or holds religious revivals
84.	SANGUINE	Cheerfully optimistic, hopeful, or confident
85.	SATYR	An evil, lascivious man; lecher
86.	SHAMBLED	Walked or went awkwardly; shuffled
87.	SINGED	Burned superficially or slightly; scorched
88.	SMITE	Strike down, injure, or slay
89.	SORDID	Filthy or dirty; foul
90.	STAGNATE	Stop developing, growing, or progressing
91.	TARNISHED	Diminished or became tainted
92.	TAWDRY	Gaudy; showy and cheap
93.	TEDIOUS	Boring, tiring, monotonous, dull
94.	TRIVIAL	Of very little importance or value; insignificant
95.	TURBID	Clouded; opaque; obscured
96.	ULSTER	Long, loose, heavy overcoat
97.	UNADULTERATED	Not mixed with impurities; without qualification
98.	UNCOUTH	Awkward, clumsy, or unmannerly
99.	VULGARITY	Act or expression that offends good taste or propriety
100.	WAINSCOTING	Wood paneling for lining interior walls

VOCABULARY WORD SEARCH - The Picture of Dorian Gray

```
D E C N O C S N E S P S R G I N F A M Y
J L N A R J B F S W E R T Y O E H P D Z
S Z W K P S S N O I Y U O T V N T A I M
B M A S D R R T L U Z N R T V I D R R K
R F I E G S I L X K N A X P E U K O U V
A F N T P R O C U R E D S I N G E D L W
C X S A E F C D E C I U E J I N E Y A A
K L C C D O Y C U D E L D R A A R S N G
E H O I H M B D R L T T P V D S H O G X
N E T D A N N O B S U E M O S N A H U F
P N I B G I S I R W L R D P I Q E T I X
O T N A G B C F O Q S A M I D D Y A D K
R R G S A U H I U A T T Y P O R Y P L L
T E U E R S U A G N E E R N O U W L Y H
I A F C D N Y R H O R D I T P M S S L M
C T F N N E C M A D T S A U E E P V D Z
O R A E E L S X M Y M V D N T L A O N T
F I W L R I F O D N R N A C U O R B U V
I V E O U C E L L E F C S O L C A E O S
A I D S S A J S S A C M P U A U S A P V
S A B N N F H N P D T T H T N T O T X X
C L V I E N O S R I S E O H T I L E E Y
O F L A C C I D A T A W D R Y O S R K X
S A T Y R R Y Z X T E B L E G L N B S B Y
E P I G R A M H E F B A L U S T R A D E
```

ABDICATE	ENTREAT	INDUCE	PROTEGE
ANODYNE	EPIGRAM	INFAMY	QUAY
ASPHODEL	ESPIAL	INSOLENCES	SANGUINE
BALUSTRADE	EXPOUND	LANGUIDLY	SATYR
BEATERS	FACILE	LURID	SINGED
BRACKEN	FETID	MYRIAD	SMITE
BROUGHAM	FIASCO	OMNIBUS	SORDID
CAPRICE	FLACCID	PARASOLS	TAWDRY
CENSURE	FOLLIES	PARODY	TEDIOUS
CONSERVATORY	FOUNDER	PATHOS	TRIVIAL
CRUCIBLE	GONDOLA	PETULANT	ULSTER
DESOLATE	GUFFAWED	POMPOUS	UNADULTERATED
DISDAIN	HAGGARD	PORTICO	UNCOUTH
ELOCUTION	HANSOM	PRATE	WAINSCOTING
ENNUI	HEDONISM	PRIG	
ENSCONCED	IDYLL	PROCURED	

VOCABULARY WORD SEARCH ANSWER KEY - The Picture of Dorian Gray

ABDICATE	ENTREAT	INDUCE	PROTEGE
ANODYNE	EPIGRAM	INFAMY	QUAY
ASPHODEL	ESPIAL	INSOLENCES	SANGUINE
BALUSTRADE	EXPOUND	LANGUIDLY	SATYR
BEATERS	FACILE	LURID	SINGED
BRACKEN	FETID	MYRIAD	SMITE
BROUGHAM	FIASCO	OMNIBUS	SORDID
CAPRICE	FLACCID	PARASOLS	TAWDRY
CENSURE	FOLLIES	PARODY	TEDIOUS
CONSERVATORY	FOUNDER	PATHOS	TRIVIAL
CRUCIBLE	GONDOLA	PETULANT	ULSTER
DESOLATE	GUFFAWED	POMPOUS	UNADULTERATED
DISDAIN	HAGGARD	PORTICO	UNCOUTH
ELOCUTION	HANSOM	PRATE	WAINSCOTING
ENNUI	HEDONISM	PRIG	
ENSCONCED	IDYLL	PROCURED	

VOCABULARY CROSSWORD The Picture Of Dorian Gray

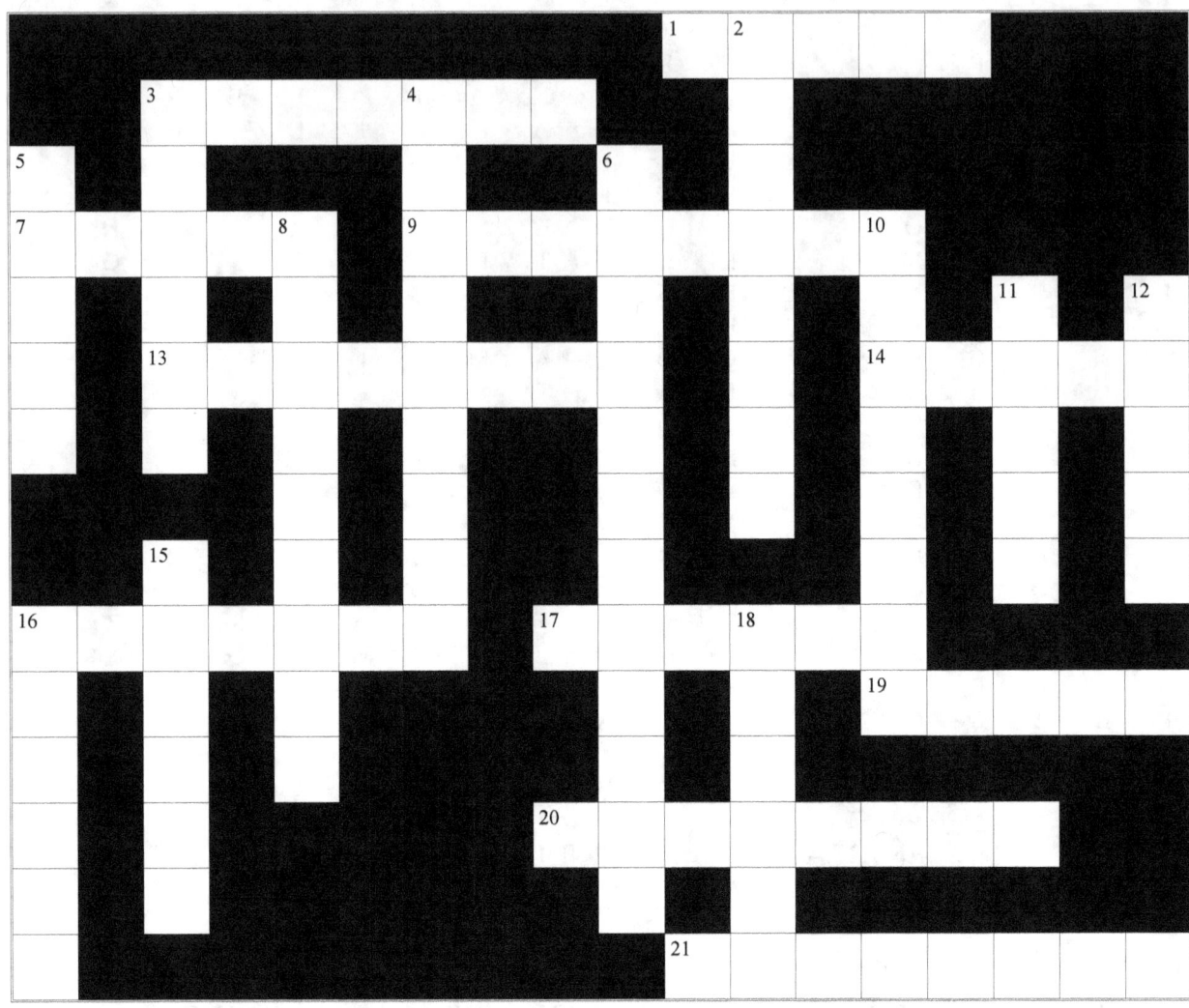

Across
1. An evil, lascivious man; lecher
3. Having a gaunt, wasted, or exhausted appearance, as from prolonged suffering, exertion, or anxiety
7. Feeling of utter weariness and discontent resulting from satiety or lack of interest; boredom
9. Devotion to pleasure as a way of life
13. Ornamental bands or borders, esp. on ecclesiastical vestments
14. Gruesome; horrible; revolting
16. Foolishness
17. Easily done, performed, or used
19. Strike down, injure, or slay
20. Closed four-wheeled carriage with an open driver's seat in the front
21. Unreasonably irritable or ill-tempered

Down
2. Renounce or relinquish a throne, right, or power
3. Two-wheeled covered carriage with the driver's seat above and behind
4. Tersely phrased statements of truth or opinion; adages
5. Having an offensive odor; stinking
6. Greenhouse, usually attached to a dwelling
8. Without emotion; apathetic; unmoved
10. Undesirable conditions or disorders
11. Talk excessively and pointlessly; babble
12. Simple descriptive or narrative piece in verse or prose
15. Long, loose, heavy overcoat
16. Complete and humiliting failure
18. To bring about, produce, or cause

VOCABULARY CROSSWORD KEY The Picture Of Dorian Gray

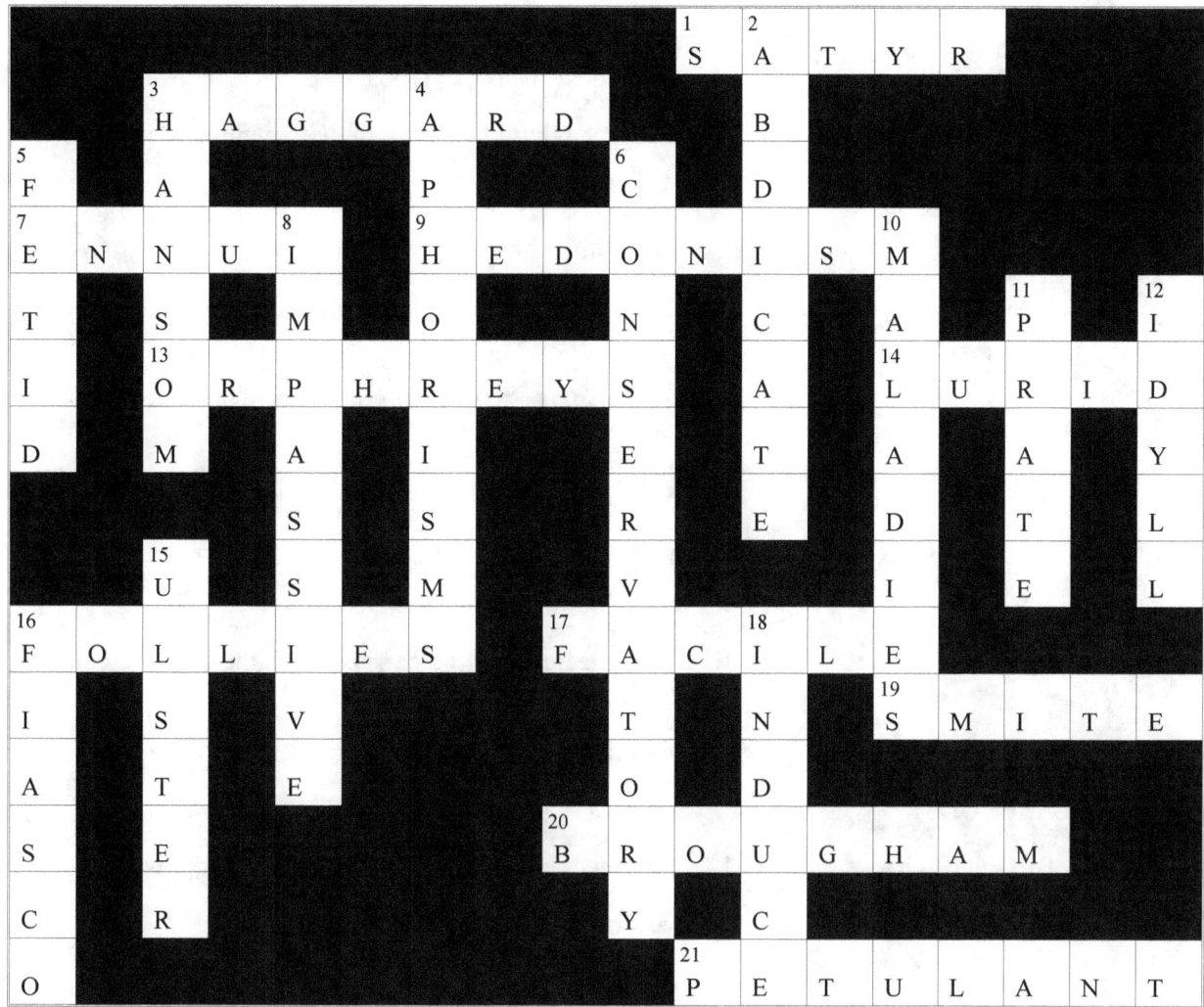

Across
1. An evil, lascivious man; lecher
3. Having a gaunt, wasted, or exhausted appearance, as from prolonged suffering, exertion, or anxiety
7. Feeling of utter weariness and discontent resulting from satiety or lack of interest; boredom
9. Devotion to pleasure as a way of life
13. Ornamental bands or borders, esp. on ecclesiastical vestments
14. Gruesome; horrible; revolting
16. Foolishness
17. Easily done, performed, or used
19. Strike down, injure, or slay
20. Closed four-wheeled carriage with an open driver's seat in the front
21. Unreasonably irritable or ill-tempered

Down
2. Renounce or relinquish a throne, right, or power
3. Two-wheeled covered carriage with the driver's seat above and behind
4. Tersely phrased statements of truth or opinion; adages
5. Having an offensive odor; stinking
6. Greenhouse, usually attached to a dwelling
8. Without emotion; apathetic; unmoved
10. Undesirable conditions or disorders
11. Talk excessively and pointlessly; babble
12. Simple descriptive or narrative piece in verse or prose
15. Long, loose, heavy overcoat
16. Complete and humiliating failure
18. To bring about, produce, or cause

VOCABULARY MATCHING 1 *The Picture of Dorian Gray*

____ 1. ABDICATE	A. Long, loose, heavy overcoat

____ 2. LIVERIES	B. State of having little or no money; penniless; poor

____ 3. MISANTHROPE	C. Contemptuously rude or impertinent behavior or speech

____ 4. PARASOLS	D. Foolishness

____ 5. POMPOUS	E. Characterized by excessive self-esteem or exaggerated dignity

____ 6. PRIG	F. Light, usually small umbrellas carried as protection from the sun

____ 7. QUAY	G. Feeling of contempt for anything regarded as unworthy

____ 8. SHAMBLED	H. Walked or went awkwardly; shuffled

____ 9. TARNISHED	I. Uniforms worn by servants

____ 10. INSOLENCES	J. Two-wheeled covered carriage with the driver's seat above and behind

____ 11. IMPECUNIOSITY	K. Diminished or became tainted

____ 12. ASPHODEL	L. Set forth or state in detail

____ 13. BROUGHAM	M. Renounce or relinquish a throne, right, or power

____ 14. CORROBORATIVE	N. Various plants of the lily family

____ 15. DISDAIN	O. Landing place constructed along the edge of a body of water

____ 16. ENSCONCED	P. Settled securely or snugly

____ 17. EXPOUND	Q. Self-righteous person who demands pointless conformity

____ 18. FOLLIES	R. Closed four-wheeled carriage with an open driver's seat in the front

____ 19. HANSOM	S. Serving to support or to make more certain

____ 20. ULSTER	T. Hater of humankind

VOCABULARY MATCHING 1 ANSWER KEY *The Picture of Dorian Gray*

M	1.	ABDICATE	A.	Long, loose, heavy overcoat
I	2.	LIVERIES	B.	State of having little or no money; penniless; poor
T	3.	MISANTHROPE	C.	Contemptuously rude or impertinent behavior or speech
F	4.	PARASOLS	D.	Foolishness
E	5.	POMPOUS	E.	Characterized by excessive self-esteem or exaggerated dignity
Q	6.	PRIG	F.	Light, usually small umbrellas carried as protection from the sun
O	7.	QUAY	G.	Feeling of contempt for anything regarded as unworthy
H	8.	SHAMBLED	H.	Walked or went awkwardly; shuffled
K	9.	TARNISHED	I.	Uniforms worn by servants
C	10.	INSOLENCES	J.	Two-wheeled covered carriage with the driver's seat above and behind
B	11.	IMPECUNIOSITY	K.	Diminished or became tainted
N	12.	ASPHODEL	L.	Set forth or state in detail
R	13.	BROUGHAM	M.	Renounce or relinquish a throne, right, or power
S	14.	CORROBORATIVE	N.	Various plants of the lily family
G	15.	DISDAIN	O.	Landing place constructed along the edge of a body of water
P	16.	ENSCONCED	P.	Settled securely or snugly
L	17.	EXPOUND	Q.	Self-righteous person who demands pointless conformity
D	18.	FOLLIES	R.	Closed four-wheeled carriage with an open driver's seat in the front
J	19.	HANSOM	S.	Serving to support or to make more certain
A	20.	ULSTER	T.	Hater of humankind

VOCABULARY MATCHING 2 *The Picture of Dorian Gray*

____ 1. AFFINITY
____ 2. LANGUIDLY
____ 3. MEDIOCRITY
____ 4. PANEGYRIC
____ 5. PHILANTHROPY
____ 6. PRESENTIMENT
____ 7. PRUDENCE
____ 8. SATYR
____ 9. STAGNATE
____ 10. INFAMY
____ 11. IMPASSIVE
____ 12. APHORISMS
____ 13. BRACKEN
____ 14. CONSERVATORY
____ 15. DESOLATE
____ 16. ENNUI
____ 17. ESPIAL
____ 18. FLACCID
____ 19. HAGGARD
____ 20. TURBID

A. State of being ordinary; not outstanding
B. In a manner lacking in spirit or interest; listlessly; indifferently
C. Feeling of evil to come
D. Having a gaunt, wasted, or exhausted appearance, as from prolonged suffering, exertion, or anxiety
E. Without emotion; apathetic; unmoved
F. Clouded; opaque; obscured
G. Stop developing, growing, or progressing
H. Caution with regard to practical matters; discretion
I. Soft and limp; not firm; flabby
J. Formal or elaborate praise
K. An evil, lascivious man; lecher
L. Extremly bad reputation
M. Greenhouse, usually attached to a dwelling
N. Natural liking for or attraction to a person, thing, idea, etc.
O. Feeling of utter weariness and discontent resulting from satiety or lack of interest; boredom
P. Feeling abandoned; forlorn
Q. Tersely phrased statements of truth or opinion; adages
R. Area overgrown with ferns and shrubs
S. Act of watching, especially in secret
T. Effort or inclination to increase the well-being of humankind

VOCABULARY MATCHING 2 ANSWER KEY *The Picture of Dorian Gray*

N	1.	AFFINITY	A.	State of being ordinary; not outstanding
B	2.	LANGUIDLY	B.	In a manner lacking in spirit or interest; listlessly; indifferently
A	3.	MEDIOCRITY	C.	Feeling of evil to come
J	4.	PANEGYRIC	D.	Having a gaunt, wasted, or exhausted appearance, as from prolonged suffering, exertion, or anxiety
T	5.	PHILANTHROPY	E.	Without emotion; apathetic; unmoved
C	6.	PRESENTIMENT	F.	Clouded; opaque; obscured
H	7.	PRUDENCE	G.	Stop developing, growing, or progressing
K	8.	SATYR	H.	Caution with regard to practical matters; discretion
G	9.	STAGNATE	I.	Soft and limp; not firm; flabby
L	10.	INFAMY	J.	Formal or elaborate praise
E	11.	IMPASSIVE	K.	An evil, lascivious man; lecher
Q	12.	APHORISMS	L.	Extremly bad reputation
R	13.	BRACKEN	M.	Greenhouse, usually attached to a dwelling
M	14.	CONSERVATORY	N.	Natural liking for or attraction to a person, thing, idea, etc.
P	15.	DESOLATE	O.	Feeling of utter weariness and discontent resulting from satiety or lack of interest; boredom
O	16.	ENNUI	P.	Feeling abandoned; forlorn
S	17.	ESPIAL	Q.	Tersely phrased statements of truth or opinion; adages
I	18.	FLACCID	R.	Area overgrown with ferns and shrubs
D	19.	HAGGARD	S.	Act of watching, especially in secret
F	20.	TURBID	T.	Effort or inclination to increase the well-being of humankind

VOCABULARY JUGGLE LETTER 1 *The Picture of Dorian Gray*

_____ = 1. STINNAIHELA
Destroys completely

_____ = 2. FRICAYOGPL
Reckless extravagance

_____ = 3. IPCPECRIE
Cliff with a vertical or overhanging face

_____ = 4. UENATTLP
Unreasonably irritable or ill-tempered

_____ = 5. OBMISUN
Vehicle carrying many passengers, used for public transport

_____ = 6. TAECLUVIR
Producing wealth; profitable

_____ = 7. ENBIILCRIGOR
Difficult or impossible to control or manage

_____ = 8. LOITDSUAOR
Having excessive or blind adoration, reverence, or devotion

_____ = 9. FICOSA
Complete and humiliting failure

_____ = 10. RIEMGPA
Concise, clever, often paradoxical statement

_____ = 11. SDENIGAGED
Freed from an engagement, pledge, or obligation

_____ = 12. URYCEHAEDB
Excessive indulgence in sensual pleasures

_____ = 13. RSOUCENCETJ
Judgments based on inconclusive or incomplete evidence

_____ = 14. AONTEENTM
Amends or reparation made for an injury or wrong

_____ = 15. ASVIELRVTI
Person who promotes or holds religious revivals

VOCABULARY JUGGLE LETTER 1 ANSWER KEY *The Picture of Dorian Gray*

ANNIHILATES	= 1.	STINNAIHELA Destroys completely
PROFLIGACY	= 2.	FRICAYOGPL Reckless extravagance
PRECIPICE	= 3.	IPCPECRIE Cliff with a vertical or overhanging face
PETULANT	= 4.	UENATTLP Unreasonably irritable or ill-tempered
OMNIBUS	= 5.	OBMISUN Vehicle carrying many passengers, used for public transport
LUCRATIVE	= 6.	TAECLUVIR Producing wealth; profitable
INCORRIGIBLE	= 7.	ENBIILCRIGOR Difficult or impossible to control or manage
IDOLATROUS	= 8.	LOITDSUAOR Having excessive or blind adoration, reverence, or devotion
FIASCO	= 9.	FICOSA Complete and humiliting failure
EPIGRAM	= 10.	RIEMGPA Concise, clever, often paradoxical statement
DISENGAGED	= 11.	SDENIGAGED Freed from an engagement, pledge, or obligation
DEBAUCHERY	= 12.	URYCEHAEDB Excessive indulgence in sensual pleasures
CONJECTURES	= 13.	RSOUCENCETJ Judgments based on inconclusive or incomplete evidence
ATONEMENT	= 14.	AONTEENTM Amends or reparation made for an injury or wrong
REVIVALIST	= 15.	ASVIELRVTI Person who promotes or holds religious revivals

VOCABULARY MATCHING 2 *The Picture of Dorian Gray*

_____ = 1. BASEADLRTU
Railing at the side of a staircase or balcony

_____ = 2. OSUITDE
Boring, tiring, monotonous, dull

_____ = 3. DDISOR
Filthy or dirty; foul

_____ = 4. ISENAGNU
Cheerfully optimistic, hopeful, or confident

_____ = 5. ORRUDPCE
Obtained or gotten by care, effort, or the use of special means

_____ = 6. SPOHTA
Feeling of sympathy or pity

_____ = 7. DPROAY
Imitate for purposes of ridicule or satire

_____ = 8. EALSMADI
Undesirable conditions or disorders

_____ = 9. MBILENNAIETR
Seeming to be without an end; endless

_____ = 10. INNAAOCNTIR
Assumption of human form or nature

_____ = 11. UFNORDE
Fill with water and sink

_____ = 12. ELRTALNH
Captivate or charm

_____ = 13. OUILENTCO
Person's manner of speaking or reading aloud in public

_____ = 14. OENRADAIGDT
A decline to a lower condition, quality, or level

_____ = 15. URNDUTAEEALDT
Not mixed with impurities; without qualification

VOCABULARY MATCHING 2 ANSWER KEY *The Picture of Dorian Gray*

BALUSTRADE	= 1.	BASEADLRTU Railing at the side of a staircase or balcony
TEDIOUS	= 2.	OSUITDE Boring, tiring, monotonous, dull
SORDID	= 3.	DDISOR Filthy or dirty; foul
SANGUINE	= 4.	ISENAGNU Cheerfully optimistic, hopeful, or confident
PROCURED	= 5.	ORRUDPCE Obtained or gotten by care, effort, or the use of special means
PATHOS	= 6.	SPOHTA Feeling of sympathy or pity
PARODY	= 7.	DPROAY Imitate for purposes of ridicule or satire
MALADIES	= 8.	EALSMADI Undesirable conditions or disorders
INTERMINABLE	= 9.	MBILENNAIETR Seeming to be without an end; endless
INCARNATION	= 10.	INNAAOCNTIR Assumption of human form or nature
FOUNDER	= 11.	UFNORDE Fill with water and sink
ENTHRALL	= 12.	ELRTALNH Captivate or charm
ELOCUTION	= 13.	OUILENTCO Person's manner of speaking or reading aloud in public
DEGRADATION	= 14.	OENRADAIGDT A decline to a lower condition, quality, or level
UNADULTERATED	= 15.	URNDUTAEEALDT Not mixed with impurities; without qualification

www.ingramcontent.com/pod-product-compliance
Lightning Source LLC
Chambersburg PA
CBHW051403070526
44584CB00023B/3270